In the Hands of the People

This is what the Lord asks of you; to act justly, love tenderly and walk humbly with your God.

(MICAH 6:8)

In the Hands of the People

Phil, Jim and Pat.

Looking forward to our paths crossing in the years to come.

Long may your light shine.
Phil ♪♪

A NEW VISION OF CHURCH

Phil Brennan

PRIMAVERA PUBLICATIONS

First published in 2014 by
Primavera Publications
Ardkeen Village
Waterford
All rights © 2014 Phil Brennan

Paperback	ISBN: 978-1-909483-65-1
Ebook – mobi format	ISBN: 978-1-909483-66-8
Ebook – ePub format	ISBN: 978-1-909483-67-5
CreateSpace	ISBN: 978-1-909483-68-2

Produced by Kazoo Publishing Services
222 Beech Park, Lucan, Co. Dublin
www.kazoopublishing.com

Kazoo Publishing Services is not the publisher of this work. All rights and responsibilities pertaining to this work remain with Primavera Publications.

Kazoo offers independent authors a full range of publishing services. For further details visit www.kazoopublishing.com

Cover design by Redsox Media
Printed in the EU

Contents

Acknowledgements

This wee book has been years in the crafting and owes its inspiration to many people who have left a deep imprint on my life and on my convictions. Many of these people fly below the radar, work humbly away from the limelight, yet give witness to all that is good in humanity. I am indebted to the following persons whose wisdom and encouragement have steered me on my course and have shaped the vision of Church that has evolved through this process. Words cannot adequately express my deep gratitude for the many ways in which you have helped me to make this aspiration a reality:

To my mother Ann whose belief in me has never waned. Her constant support and friendship has been the source of great strength and has encouraged me through each step of my journey.

To my family and friends for keeping my feet firmly rooted on the ground and for making sure that I never took myself or my writing too seriously. Whether it was the quiet chats, the tasty meals, the rounds of golf, the games of cards, the camaraderie and the laughs; these experiences have helped me to find the reserves necessary to see things through. A special thanks to the Funges in Gorey, to Jo and Tom Fitzgerald and Gerry Horan on the Cork Road, Waterford, to Drew and Linda Hamilton in Omagh and my extended choir family, to Sr. Phyllis and Sr. June in the Ursuline Community, Waterford, to Declan Kelly, Don Devine, Leo Walsh, Helen McGrath, Janet Carey, Jim Sheehan, Alan Kinsella, Sean McEvoy, Elaine Harvey and all who helped me in so many ways along the way.

To my PhD supervisor Michael Howlett and my examiners Pauline Logue and Michael O'Sullivan for their painstaking guidance and support. Their depth of insight and their clarity of vision always pointed me in the right direction.

To the Christian Brothers in The Edmund Rice Heritage Centre, Waterford whose generosity of spirit knows no bounds. Kevin, Phil, Peadar, Addie, John, Seamus, Pat and Steve all testify to the compassion and courage of their founder, Blessed Edmund Rice, in all that they do.

To the theologians, social justice activists, members of social justice groups and small Christian communities who provided that vital 'spark' that helped to ground the theology in the everyday. A particular thanks to Gemma McKenna, Yvonne Daly and Mary McQuaide from 'The Fig Tree Group' for the warmth of their welcome to Fatima Mansions and for introducing me to the unique dynamics of a small Christian community. My genuine indebtedness also to Donal Dorr, Peter McVerry, Maria McGuinness, James O' Halloran and Martin Byrne for sharing their unique perspective on the challenges facing the Church at this time. These people capture what is of lasting value as much through their deeds as through their words.

To my dad Phil whose guiding spirit has led me to this point. I dedicate this book to his memory.

Introduction
A Time for Change

The sun rose, it glistened across the hardened landscape and the cold morning mist was eclipsed by a compelling warmth that seeped through all who were present. St. Peter's Square at 10am on a January morning is not the warmest of places. Yet, as Pope Francis meandered his way through the multitudes, there was a very palpable sense that something new was happening under the sun. A spirit beyond the narrow parameters of what the mind can fully absorb was at play. Rarely have I witnessed such an outpouring of hope. People's eyes were transfixed on a man whose smile radiated far and wide. The mood was uplifting. In an instant, we were transported outside our normal boundaries. Daniela, an Italian woman I'd never met before, asked if I could e-mail her my photos. A common humanity was forged. Can this man really herald the beginning of something new?

I couldn't help but feel that Pope Francis recognises that the future of the Catholic Church lies not in the corridors of power and authority but on the fringes, among those once consigned to the periphery. Could his embrace of the many children that were passed into his arms signal the advent of a new time of possibility, a time when those in elevated positions reach out to those who are most vulnerable and voiceless, and, together with them, carve out a new face of Church in the world today. Pope Francis deflects from himself onto others. The mantle is being passed on to the people.

Momentarily, I was able to forget the reality of the Church that I had left behind in Ireland. The institutional Church here has lost its way, and, in so doing, continues to occupy some esoteric realm far removed from the day to day concerns of the people it claims to serve. Church liturgies often fail to connect with the experiences of people and the enduring resonance of the Gospel seems somewhat obscured against the opaque backdrop of existing rituals. People are increasingly alienated in a world of ecclesial protocol and liturgical correctness. Many have walked away, some remain. All recognise that the Church as an institution has deviated from its intended path and has become a dim reflection of everything it was meant to be.

There are parishes that beat to a different rhythm and create an opening for the people, in partnership with their priests, to breathe new life into the Church's mission in their midst. In these places, the people are not simply recipients of the Christian story; they become bearers of the timeless truths contained within its pages. Traditional divisions dissipate in a climate of dialogue and cooperation as the stifling ways of the past surrender to something more liberating. Equally, there are priests, bishops, sisters and brothers wearing themselves out in the service of others, walking in solidarity with the young and the old, the marginalised and those struggling to cope with the adversities of today. Have these many good men and women who embody the true spirit of the Gospel been betrayed by a system that has lost touch with its soul?

The residual scar of the child sex abuse scandal in the Church and the unimaginable hurt it has wreaked continues to damage the credibility of Church authorities the world over. Recent revelations in Ireland have lifted the lid on a shameful chapter in the history of the Catholic Church here and the disturbing truths that they disclose scream at us and tell us that we have no choice but to change course. The shocking nature of these crimes is further amplified by the subsequent cover-up and both are symptomatic of a deeper malaise within the Church. The fact that this abuse went undetected for so long exposes the anomalies of an ecclesial mindset that places blind allegiance and loyalty above all other considerations. Could it be that, for some, subservience to the prevailing model of governance supersedes any genuine attempt to reach the truth and to hold the perpetrators accountable for their actions?

In the meantime, the story of the carpenter from Nazareth has all but slipped from our view and the true identity of the Church in the world remains dimmed and compromised beyond recognition. Is this the legacy of our Christian heritage that we hand on to future generations? The inclination to prop up and protect the established order must give way to a willingness to promote the radical reform that this abuse necessitates. The plea for forgiveness from the hierarchy, no matter how genuine, only becomes credible if it is matched by a clear resolve to overhaul the system that permitted, and often camouflaged, these crimes in the first place.

What is required then is a seismic shift in how authority is exercised so that leaders in the Catholic Church begin to listen to the voices of those whose experiences and insights have remained largely unheeded until now. A new perspective needs to filter through the veins of an institution deeply hostile to the democratic process. Individuals who raise their head above the parapet are met with stiff resistance. It seems incredulous that in recent years five Irish priests have been silenced for encouraging discussion on issues of celibacy, women priests and homosexuality. In a climate of intimidation and denunciation, free thinking, no matter how well intentioned, is dismissed as misguided and subversive. It is time for a new mindset, for "a conscious release from traditionalism in order to keep the tradition alive and meaningful" (Haight, 2001:xii). Leadership involves daring to venture outside the safe havens of the past and seizing the opportunities that this moment in history presents before they are lost. To take that step is not an act of betrayal; more a defiant signal that all need not necessarily remain the same. A lot of what is there now must be shed, must die before we move on. The Church must undergo its own 'chrysalis', for only in the shedding of the old can the present bring us closer to the possibilities of the future.

The moment of truth has arrived. The movement of the Church through the ages has reached a decisive crossroads. Rather than merely repeating the ways of the past, Church leaders need to journey alongside their people and set out on uncharted roads without knowing the risks and obstacles that will be encountered along the way. Pope Francis calls us to reach out beyond our present experience of Church and anticipate previously unexplored avenues so that "instead of looking back, there is a focus on the future, on where we want to and must go" (Pope Francis, 2013:143). The true pathway the Church must traverse is discovered by listening to the hidden voices of the 'unlikely' ones, the indivisible human compass that draws the institution back closer to its source and to its people. At the grassroots, something is stirring, something altogether different from what has gone before. A new awakening is happening. People are starting to recognise that whilst the hierarchy are an integral part of the Church, they are not the entirety of it. What we are witnessing on the periphery is a myriad of "extra-institutional spaces" (Ganiel, 2012:43) as people begin to leave their own imprint on the style of Church that they want to be part of. An eclectic mix of prayer groups, social justice and ecology organisations, meditation workshops, spirituality seminars, Gospel choirs, all form part of a new landscape of Church that is ever so gradually evolving on the margins.

Out of the embers of the past, the Church we aspire towards is slowly taking shape before our very eyes. Pushed to the edge of the precipice, those on the sidelines of the old order are unravelling the layers of what it means to be Church and are penetrating through to the core of what is important. It is here on the fringes that we begin to see the Church mirror within itself the humility of its origins as it echoes resolutely to the heartbeat of its people. Times demand of us a clear resolve to tap into the dynamism that is palpable at the grassroots, and, in dialogue with the people, "re-examine what it means to be church, imagine a new vision and begin to take the steps to implement this vision" (O'Hanlon, 2011:9). This book attempts to do just that!

To where do we turn for inspiration? Over the past fifty years, a new dynamic of Church has emerged out of Latin America that blazes a trail for the universal Church to follow.

Given the Spanish name *Communidades Ecclesiales de Base*, Base Christian Communities, this cluster of small Christian communities comprise of the people at the 'base' of society, as opposed to those who occupy positions closer to the pinnacle of power on the social pyramid. Power percolates from the people upwards and each person becomes integral to the life and governance of their local faith community: "The support of community is essential for the crossing of the desert. So true is this that only in community can one travel this road" (Gutiérrez, 2005:133). These communities are not an alternative Church but a more credible Church as those once silenced in society channel their collective energy to bring the liberating power of the Gospel to life. Each community is sustained from within but projects outward and strengthens the resolve of the people to overcome what is intolerable in their surroundings: "The periphery is the vessel of hope, the bearer of the future ... Slowly, stubbornly, faith is taking flesh in our countries and acquiring a new face. A new way of being Christian is being tested" (Boff, 1989:8).

The theologians of liberation provide a unique theological backdrop against which the defining features of this emerging model of Church can be explored. The ambit of inquiry is widened to include the insights and observations of theologians and activists beyond Latin America who speak from experience of the unique appeal of the small Christian community. This book moves from the past, to the present and on to the future; from exploring the origins of the prevailing structures in the Church and critiquing their limitations, to assessing how the dynamic of small Christian community re-defines what it means to be Church in the world today with a specific spotlight on how it translates into an Irish setting, to pointing towards practical strategies that can give real impetus to the activity of the Church in each new time and place. The themes are developed in clearly sequenced episodes and each needs time to 'sit' and be absorbed before the reader moves on to the next. The unique legacy of Archbishop Óscar Romero is explored towards the end of the book and offers a new perspective on the path the Church must take if it is to re-discover its true identity in the world.

Theological insight is arrived at not in isolation from all that is revealed in each new age but in correspondence with the distinctive flair of people at the grassroots to capture what lies at the essence of the Church's mission in the world. The Christian story and the story of the people on the margins converge to signal a new way forward. The intent is not to undermine and devalue the role of the institutional Church, more to see how the creative reserves of its people can transform it. The momentum for change is slowly gathering pace. It will not be subdued.

> *Courage must lead us not to half way reforms that badly gloss over our fears and trepidations, but to a transformation of what we know today ... times demand of us a creative spark that will allow us to think up and create new ecclesial structures and new ways for the Christian Community to be present in the world.*
>
> (GUTIÉRREZ, 1983:34)

Seizing the Moment
A Visual Overview

I stared in disbelief and a suffocating anguish came over me. Like sporadic images on a reel, memories from my past cascaded down the dismal walls of my surrounds. The engulfing torrent overwhelmed me and cast doubts on my capacity to wade my way to the other side. Imprisoned within a darkened world, hope flickered tremulously before the warmth of its glow seemed to fade. The future I once aspired towards dissolved abruptly into the chilling canvas of a sombre sky. In an instant, all had changed.

Moments of trial suspend the graspable contours of everyday and lure us into the inner recesses of our being. It is here, stripped of all that once defined us, we come to discover who we really are. Such is the paradox of life; suffering can become a gateway to truth, a channel into the unknown. Through the obscurity, what once escaped us now becomes clear: "Often we have to come to the edge of the precipice before we reach the moment of truth and recognise our own poverty and need of each other, and cry to God for help ... Times of trial release new energies" (Vanier, 1979:76-77). A voice cries in the wilderness of our existence and reminds us that we are not alone. There is an indivisible thread woven through the world of human experience that draws us into the vast expanse of mystery. Our hour of crisis opens the pores of our humanity to the mystical power of love and amidst the rubble and the brokenness, a faint hope is re-kindled. The storm clouds part and the landscape, though somewhat tinged by pain, glows with a hue we never noticed before.

The Church too is staring into the abyss and is timorously delving into its inner depths in search of enlightenment. The spectre of its recent history casts a shadow on the legacy being handed on to future generations. We now stand on the precipice. Will the Church find within itself the reserves necessary to resist the tumult or will it drift irreversibly towards its demise? Today, there is a need for fresh energies in a Church grown weary. This time of trial can open the floodgates of the institution to a redemptive current, to the life force of its own people. You see, the Church was never meant to elevate itself above the world and remain somewhat aloof and removed from the cut and thrust of history. Rather, the Church evolves in symmetry with the efforts of its people to advance in each new age God's intentions for humanity: "The church is forever moving forward and must always explore new ways to bring the love of God into others' lives" (Mannion, 2007:209).

Love bridges the seamless ties between humanity and God. This truth, once discovered, changes everything. A Church embedded in the struggles and joys of its people reverberates to the beat of God's love. The receding tide creates the space for something new to follow. Maybe, just maybe, the present crisis can become "a favourable time, a kairos ... a special period of God's saving action, a time when a new route is being carved out for the following of Jesus" (Gutiérrez, 2005:20). Can the institutional Church reach outside its sheltered boundaries and begin to forge an enduring solidarity with its people? The scale of this challenge cannot be understated, equally the magnitude of the reward. It is a time of perennial significance, a moment of truth that could resonate long into the future. It takes courage to take the first tentative steps towards freedom. To dare is to believe in the possibility of something better!

Daring to
Break Free

The Church is not fossilised in the past, immovable and unchanging, but is an ongoing movement that reflects the vagaries of time. It is very much shaped by the historical nuances of each new age. All that now exists has been centuries in the making! The rituals and structures acquired from the hallowed vaults of bygone eras are part of the fabric of what we know today. Somewhere along the line, the hierarchy became intrinsic to the identity of the Church and a dynamic of power that flows from the top downward became absolute. In the process, the system usurped the story and the message became blurred. The time has come to open up the shutters of tradition to the creative energy unique to each new generation and discover in the inordinate spirit of the people those very qualities needed to sustain the Church as it moves forward. Blind homage to the past must give way to something new: "The surest, safest route for today is not the pathway to the past – the road already travelled. The surest, safest route for us today is the still-emblazoned trail leading straight ahead and to the future" (Boff, 1989:32).

How did the Church come to deviate so far from its intended path? The origins of what we have today can be traced back to centuries-old patterns, arising from its close association with Roman power and the feudal structure. The imprint of the past is very much in the present: "It is necessary to soberly and precisely analyse this Roman system to discover whether the Catholic Church could not, perhaps, be saved if it ceased to be enslaved to this system" (Küng, 2013:64). The Church assumed customs, titles, regulations, even symbols from the distinctive style of governance deployed by the Roman Empire to protect its realm. Hierarchy, as a term and as a concept, is a result of this process. Under this system, the hierarchy has distinct 'orders' or tiers of authority that increase in importance as you move upwards. The one in a position of supremacy is effectively such for life and his will is law. Power is ordained from above, from the will of God, and the authority bestowed on a privileged few cannot come under the scrutiny of anyone from below: "The higher someone is in this hierarchy the closer one is to God and so has a greater share in God's divine power ... A questioning from below would be equal to a revolution in the universe. Thus, any thought of transformation is the same as an attack on God" (Boff, 1985:41).

Within this framework, power is inherited directly from Christ, transmitted initially to the Apostles and then to their successive bishops, cardinals and popes down through the centuries. Pronouncements from on high are considered irrefutable and unquestionable and the people duly obey! Heavy levels of conformity are imposed and allegiance to the prevailing system implies protecting and safeguarding its established norms: "The top officers are regarded as servants of the institution, bound by a rigid party line, unresponsive to the legitimate religious concerns of the faithful ... At the risk of caricature, one may say that many think of the Church as a huge, impersonal machine set over and against its own members" (Dulles, 1983:3).

This dynamic of governance, by its nature, is self-perpetuating; it resists all forces opposed to its existence. Preserving the status quo supersedes all other considerations and the relentless march of those in command condemns the majority to the sidelines. Power is contained within the hierarchical cosmos and anyone outside this domain languishes in the shadows. The resulting polarity between those in authority and those in obedience discourages participation on the part of those on the lower tiers of the pyramid: "In terms of decision, the participation of the faithful is totally mutilated. Decision is restricted to the pope-bishop-pastor axis. A community in which the routes of participation are cut off in all directions cannot pretend to the name of community" (Boff, 1997:30). The dominant pattern of rule that we have inherited from the past has become normalised to a point that it seems to most people that 'the Church' equals 'the institutional or clerical church'. Under these constraints, "the activity of lay Christians appears to be marginal to what the Church is about; and if it becomes significant it is almost immediately taken under clerical control" (Dorr, 2004:231).

Women remain anonymous and devalued within a system that stifles rather than liberates their true potential. Few regimes in the world so flagrantly ignore the rights of women as the institutional Church; birth control is prohibited, decision-making on matters of importance lies beyond their sphere of influence and ordination remains the exclusive privilege of men only. Despite the irreplaceable participation of women in the founding and the spread of the Church, women have had no voice over the centuries in articulating the Church's doctrine, moral teaching and law. They have been denied their rightful place at the table. Their efforts to promote change are rendered obsolete in a male-dominated bureaucracy that will not yield. Surely, the status quo is neither just nor sustainable. The model of Church passed down through the ages has become estranged from the source of its renewal: "The most important criteria for church office should no longer be male gender and opportunistic, conformist affirmation of the *status quo*" but rather "the development of a community based on a real partnership of men and women in the Church" (Küng, 2013:305).

Today, a new voice is seeping through the fault lines and beginning to make itself heard. The flaws of the current dynamic of Church have never been so pronounced and the myth of clericalism that has propped up the traditional Church for so long has finally exploded. In the wake of the clerical abuse scandal, the passive, subservient attitude towards the people at the top is gradually being replaced by the stoic resolve of growing numbers to transform what is no longer tolerable, regardless of the resistance. The lid has been lifted on the anomalies of a bureaucracy that has paid scant regard to the wellbeing of those most vulnerable and voiceless under its care.

Many clergy and members of religious congregations too struggle for clarity in the face of great confusion and uncertainty. They live with the taint of crimes perpetrated by others and unfairly so. The Association of Catholic Priests (ACP) was founded with a view to promoting a new climate of dialogue in the Catholic Church in Ireland. Whilst the hierarchy here is reluctant to actively engage in this process, the ACP remains committed to "restructuring the governing system of the Church, basing it on service rather than on power, and encouraging at every level a culture of consultation and transparency" (Association of Catholic Priests, 2012). The remnants of the traditional order are coming under closer scrutiny than ever before. It is all too apparent that the Church has become something it was never meant to be. Recognising this cold truth is the first step on the long road to freedom!

Yet, what has evolved over centuries will not simply disappear overnight. Dismantling the barriers of clericalism will take time! Some cling obstinately to the prevailing norms and fail to see outside their narrow boundaries. They become hostage to a certain ambition to 'climb up the ladder', and, as they ascend upwards, become reluctant to relinquish or share their power and privilege: "The hierarchy themselves, according to this view are prisoners of the system they impose on others" (Dulles, 1983:3). Lay people who are seeking genuine reform find themselves increasingly alienated within an institution that effectively imposes its own limits on the scope of this reform. Within the parameters of the current structures, permission for any new course of action must be sanctioned by the local priest or bishop if it is to have legitimacy. The powers attributed to people in parish councils are largely ineffective given that their decisions can ultimately be vetoed by those in authority beyond the council. In the meantime, numbers attending mass continue to dwindle, vocations slow down to a virtual halt and those submerged in the system remain oblivious to the scale of its shortcomings. Pope Francis calls for a time when leaders and the people alike reach out beyond the insular confines of the traditionalist mindset in search of new horizons: "Tradition and memory of the past must help us to have the courage to open up new areas to God ... those who stubbornly try to recover a past that no longer exists – they have a static and inward-directed view of things" (Pope Francis, 2013:11).

Re-configuring what it means to be Church is a matter of great urgency. The people must provide the creative spark necessary to activate the process of reform. Transformation that flows from the base upwards is more likely to endure as it reflects the interests of the entire Church and not just the chosen few at the top of the ecclesial pyramid. The world we live in teaches us that when disempowered peoples channel their collective energies to promote change, anything is possible. What we are witnessing is a radical shift towards new forms of democracy in places of great political upheaval. The recent history of El Salvador, East Timor and Burma, to name but a few, testifies to the transformative potential of movements on the periphery of old dictatorial regimes in their pursuit of equality and freedom.

Their path involves much persecution and sacrifice and often reflects the ambiguities and confusions common to all struggles. Each new generation will persevere no matter how great the might of those who oppose the legitimacy of their aspirations. Their spirit will not be subdued. Congar prophetically anticipated a quarter of a century ago how the irrepressible surge towards liberation in people's movements at that time would ultimately percolate beyond the political arena into the life of the Church: "Today people no longer want to be objects but subjects... That is true in all spheres: in political life, in the Church generally and more specifically in the local churches as over against the central Roman authority" (Congar, 1988:67).

Freire's book *Pedagogy Of The Oppressed* (1970) offers a unique and timeless insight into how a once subservient people can become determining subjects in their own history and effect real change in the world, a process that is applicable to society and Church in equal measure. Freire contends that those subjected to oppressive societal forces become complicit in preserving the system of dominance by their silence and their inability to take decisive action. They acquiesce to the prevailing norms and "are inhibited from waging the struggle for freedom so long as they feel incapable of running the risks it requires" (Freire, 1970:29). Each individual needs to recognise that their social milieu is not a fixed, static entity beyond their powers of influence, but a dynamic that evolves over time in accordance with the creativity and yearnings that they bring to it: "In order for the oppressed to be able to wage the struggle for liberation, they must perceive the reality of oppression not as a closed world from which there is no exit, but as a limiting situation which they can transform" (Freire, 1970:31). This realisation, once internalised in the consciousness of the people, becomes the springboard for action. Change starts from within and radiates outwards. What emerges can liberate both the oppressed and the oppressor and can pave the way for an unlikely alliance. A new life force is unearthed from the indefatigable reserves of the people: "This, then, is the great humanistic and historical task of the oppressed: to liberate themselves and their oppressors as well ... Only power that springs from the weakness of the oppressed will be sufficiently strong to free both" (Freire, 1970:26).

The moment of truth is upon us. If the Church continues to think in terms of power and acts on the basis of that thinking, it will always reflect "the kind of unity that belongs to a faction closed in upon itself" (Rahner, 1992:244). The Church can only become a force for change in the world and remain true to its original course if it reflects this change within its own structures. Something more inclusive of all the people is required. The hour has arrived when those once silent step forward and reclaim their place in the Church. Standing on the sidelines is no longer an option!: "'Ordinary' Christians are not being faithful to the gospel if they do not expect – and even demand – that Church ministers and authorities consult with them and enable them to be actively involved in shaping and carrying out the mission of the church" (Dorr, 2004:203).

Those in authority, for their part, need to make that quantum leap and realise that a Church that walks in solidarity with its people must open the doors of the institution to their incorrigible spirit. To share in their journey is to be empowered, and indeed transformed, by all that is discovered along the way! Pope Francis recognises the challenge this presents to leaders in the Church the world over: "The people of God want pastors, not clergy acting like bureaucrats or government officials. The bishops, particularly, want to be able to support the movement of God among their people with patience, so that no one is left behind. But they must also be able to accompany the flock that has the flair for finding new paths ... that takes audacity and courage" (Pope Francis, 2013:7).

Bridging the
Great Divide

The hierarchical Church has lived in splendid isolation from the world for too long now and has lost touch with the real needs of its people. All too often, the established rituals and formulas of the past have insulated the Church from the pressing challenges posed in the present. The world of ecclesial correctness and doctrinal certainty seems a vast distance from the impoverishment and suffering that many in the world today have to endure on a daily basis. The clearly defined parameters of the traditional Church rarely extend beyond the confines of the religious sphere: "As long as the Church's mission is conceived in doctrinal terms the conflict in the world will not besmirch the Church" (Sobrino, 1984:208). At stake here is the credibility of the Church's mission in the world today.

To cling rigidly to the ways of old blinds us with indifference to the revelations of today. The ideals on which the Church is founded must find expression beyond the narrowed walls of the institution and come to life in the everyday world where the true efficacy of these ideals can be measured: "Thinking about ideals is the means to avoid becoming prey to the institutions we currently possess. Institutions embody our ideals, but our ideals are never fully exhausted by existing institutions" (Patrella, 2006:105). Christian ideals, no matter how prized, cannot be contained within an institution but need to be muddied in the harsh, abrasive realities unique to each new age if they are to impact on history. Once absorbed into the texture of today, these ideals breathe afresh and break out beyond the hardened veneer of the past. When the timeless truths we inherit come to life in our midst, we begin to project beyond our normal vantage point and see things differently: "It's a matter of plunging bravely back into our ideals, the ones that guided our history, and of starting, right now, to implement other possibilities, other values, other forms of behaviour" (Pope Francis, 2013:262).

Surely it is time to break down the artificial divide between the Church and the world and ensure that the frontiers between the two are fluid in both directions. The Church must lay down its tent among its people and here, divested of its superfluous trappings, re-discover its true identity. Through the ages, the

Church has always appeared somewhat aloof and removed from the world, preferring to superimpose its doctrines and moral pronouncements on those under its dominion from a safe distance. In his book *The Community Called Church* (1973), Segundo sheds light on how the Church was once viewed as a supernatural society, complete and juridically perfect, that passes judgment on the world from the secluded vaults of its self-imposed boundaries. It is as though the Church as an institution came to occupy some esoteric space that circumvents time and place and towered above the lowly humanity of its people. Segundo recognises that the Church cannot remain adrift from the world and immune to the struggles of those it purports to serve: "A church which dialogues and works with the rest of mankind is a church that knows she is part of humanity ... a church that knows she is, by definition, in the service of humanity" (Segundo, 1973:131).

Service, humble service, bridges the once interminable chasm between the institution and the world. Here, on the underside of history, the Church becomes susceptible to a new current, and, charged anew, takes on a brave new form: "The power of love is different in nature from the power of domination; it is fragile, vulnerable, conquering through its weakness and its capacity for giving and forgiveness" (Boff, 1985:59). Love liberates the Church from the captivity of old. In opting to descend down from its loftier heights, the institutional Church returns home to where it belongs.

The Church can no longer stand on the sidelines and remain impartial to the story of its people. Its place rests assuredly in the shadows of civilisation among the multitudes searching for meaning and direction in a world that has lost its way. On the margins, a new path has opened up as those once silent begin to leave an indelible imprint on the activity of the Church in the world. Here, somewhat below the radar, the Church walks shoulder to shoulder with its people as they come together to lend support to each other in times of trial, or to protest against the denigration of their rights and aspirations, or to highlight issues of ecological importance to their surroundings, or to empower each other through education to take the concrete steps necessary to promote change or simply to create a sacred space to sustain them on their way. In a myriad of new forms, the Gospel is laid bare among its people. The Church reveals its human face to the world and now, embedded in the struggles of humanity, discovers a more authentic way of signifying its source in history: "The church must be the visible sign of the presence of the Lord ... Only in this way will the message of love which the church bears be made credible and efficacious" (Gutiérrez, 1988:234). God's love beats through the pulse of humanity to become a palpable force in history. Sharing in the story of those most persecuted in the world makes possible our liberating encounter with God. The Church, as sacrament, now embodies the message it proclaims to the world.

The wretched social conditions endured by the world's poor are a perennial reminder that the current course of history is incomplete. Hope is a luxury that few can afford in places of dire destitution. The task of the Church is to respond to the real and pressing needs of the downtrodden with the urgency their plight necessitates. Too many people remain voiceless and alienated in a world that tramples mercilessly on their basic human needs. The salvation they seek cannot degenerate into the promise of something illusory. The Church needs to rethink its mission.

Its purpose is not simply to 'save' in the sense of guaranteeing heaven; the work of salvation occurs in history: "What saves us are not truths formulated in neat sentences but rather God himself who is given as salvation" (Boff, 1985:46). To view salvation as something other-worldly is to evade the pressing questions posed in each new age and minimise the liberating power of human interaction. The story of salvation unfolds in this world as a "set of possibilities in history, a history in which the struggle for life and liberation of millions is bound up with the responses of others also" (O'Sullivan, 1986:94). God does not operate in isolation from the world but works through humanity to create the conditions that make salvation possible. This realisation, once fully absorbed, radically re-defines what it means to be Church in the world.

The theologians of liberation place a spotlight on the unique contribution of grassroots communities to the rolling out of salvation in history. The resilience and dynamism of these communities create an opening for the divine to intervene in the finite strands of this world in a special way and "reveal to us the deep meaning of history which we fashion with our own hands" (Gutiérrez, 1973:237). The concerted efforts of these communities to effect change, no matter how understated or humble, advance in history the destiny that God intends for humanity. God's saving love becomes a potent force in the everyday occurrences that define the life of each community. The challenge this presents to Christians the world over is clear: "The ultimate possibility open to human beings is that they should live the very life of God or, in other words, do within history that which finds expression in the essential reality of God, namely, love in a way that re-creates, saves, and gives life" (Sobrino, 1984:46).

These theologians understand the essential balance that must be achieved between affirming an absolute future beyond the constraints of this world and recognising the significance of this moment in history: "The salvation that Jesus has gained and offered to us all is certainly not limited to the "end time." It overflows that time, surging back to the present" (Boff, 1989:170-171). God's love has no boundaries, and, as such, extends to all of humanity through the ages. Christian communities that bear the burdens of the weak and the impoverished, irrespective of their creed or race, move civilisation closer to the goal that ultimately God alone can deliver. The divides of the past disappear in light of this enduring truth: "The church has no walls, nor does it draw a circle around itself that separates it from the world" (Russell, 1974:158).

The Church as we once knew it is fading before our eyes and is being replaced by something radically different from what has preceded it. The resolve of the people at the grassroots to generate real hope into their surroundings has a significance that transcends the immediacy of their historical situation: "Suddenly we see: with the margin as its starting place, the gospel reveals its native colours. Our gaze is purer now. We behold only the essential. Everything becomes convincingly clear, and we are moved by the impact" (Boff, 1989:42).

Pope Francis is in no doubt that St. Francis epitomises the path the Church must take if the ideals of the Gospel are to find a more secure footing in the world: "For me, he is the man of poverty, the man of peace ... He is the man who gives us the spirit of peace, the poor man ... Oh, how I wish for a Church that is poor and for the poor" (Pope Francis, 2013:1). The poor live the truth about humanity in its barest form; what matters most is the love of the family, the dignity of holding a useful job, keeping the faith no matter how great the adversity, retaining a sense of humour in life against all the odds. The poor cultivate tiny gestures of love and care so as to safeguard the wellbeing of those most oppressed in their midst. Their spirit reflects the potential within all of us to remove the superfluous layers of life and strip everything down to the core essentials. As true prophets, the poor reveal God's design: "We need to let ourselves be evangelised by them ... to acknowledge the saving power at work in their lives and to put them at the centre of the Church's pilgrim way ... We are called to find Christ in them, to lend our voice to their causes ... to embrace the mysterious wisdom that God wishes to share with us through them" (Pope Francis, 2013:103).

Closeness to the poor re-unites the Church with what is of enduring significance. The cry of the poor echoes a subliminal cry within each one of us. We are one with them. When we reach out to our sister or brother in need, we embrace our shared humanity. We unearth from within the fundamental human impulse to love. Magaña argues that the Church *of* the poor differs distinctly from the Church *for* the poor in that it recognises their inalienable worth and their capacity to transform the life of the Church: "This is meant not only in the sense that it makes an option for them, lives for them, and is persecuted for their sake... but mainly in the sense that it arises from them, from their believing response" (Magaña, 1993:185). Communities animated by all that they encounter among the poor cannot help but dramatically change the Church today. The institution, in unison with its people, begins to find its way amidst the rubble and the brokenness: "They are directed by a new mode of living and of acting, by a new perception of reality and by a new experience of being. They emerge from a collective path, a path that is being made as we walk" (Boff, 2007:10).

The Movement
Towards Community

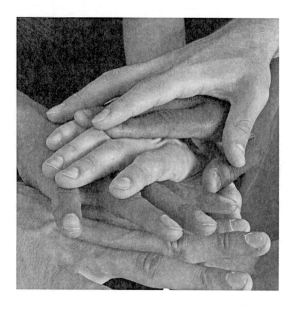

Small Christian communities provide a template for a new way of being Church in the world. Almost unannounced, those once consigned to the periphery of the Church are assuming new responsibilities and asserting themselves in ways previously unknown in communities across the globe. Ironically, the shortage of priests in parishes across Latin America over the past half century provided the stimulus needed to mobilise men and women to take up the mantle and play a more decisive role in their local faith communities.

On the outskirts of the cities, in little villages, in the immense hinterland where a priest is almost never seen, the people gather to celebrate the message of liberation and to reclaim roles denied to them during centuries of clericalism. These communities may "still be in embryonic form but we can already see in them the shape of the Church that is to come" (Boff, 1997:33). Ministries are allocated in accordance with the gifts and talents at the disposal of each community. The sum of the individual ministries contributes to the wellbeing of the whole: "Without these ministers, communities of faith are left to themselves, and run the risk of falling apart and disappearing" (Boff, 1985:125). The people have stepped in from the sidelines and the Church is being transformed by their presence: "Now there is a new doer, a new maker of history, in the church, and this new active subject is doing theology" (Ellis and Maduro, 1989:505).

The happenings at the grassroots in the *Communidades Ecclesiales de Base* over the past few decades have precipitated an era of great change in how the Church operates around the world. When the Latin American Episcopate met in Medellin, Colombia in 1968 and in Puebla de los Angeles, Mexico in 1979, they acclaimed the distinctive vibrancy of these Christian communities and recognised the intrinsic value of the laity to the life of the Church. The bishops in Medellin saw in communities at the 'base' of the Church evidence of "the initial cell of the ecclesiastical structures and the focus of evangelization ... The essential element for the existence of Christian base communities are their leaders or directors. These can be priests, deacons, men or women religious, or lay people" (Medellin Document in Boff, 1997:15). Each community was viewed as a living cell within an all-encompassing network of communities in that each cell reflected within itself something of the universal Church: "They are a new type of basic cell structure of the church, the first time in centuries that any significant sector of the church has developed new grass-roots structures for living out the faith" (Kirby, 1981:23).

Medellin anticipated a time when those silent and anonymous within the Church of old would rise up and break free from all that once impeded them. A new creative force was unleashed. The grassroots had now become the heartbeat of the Church and each community provided a vital artery between the people and the institution: "Medellin was a fundamental commitment to work for the construction of a community Church instead of the vertical Church we inherited with its pyramid of power" (Lernoux, 1979:11).

The Medellin documents reflect a decisive shift away from a centralised Church orchestrated from Rome towards more autonomous communities propelled forward by their own people. The Church is no longer a bystander to the history of those it serves but instead participates with them in their struggle for freedom: "It is necessary that small basic communities be developed in order to establish a balance with minority groups ... The church – the people of God – will lend its support to the down-trodden of every social class so that they might come to know their rights and how to make use of them" (Medellin, 1968: no. 1.20). The Church now bears the burdens of its people; co-operatives are set up to promote employment, medical services are improved to more adequately cater for the needs of the weak and the infirm and educational programmes are organised to empower the people to address the root causes of their impoverishment.

The unique dynamism of these communities and their ever widening proliferation across Latin America is celebrated in the Puebla documents as a source of great hope for the universal Church: "We are happy to single out the multiplication of small communities as an important ecclesial event that is peculiarly ours, and as the hope of the Church" (Puebla, 1978: no. 629). The bishops in Medellin and Puebla could glimpse then the dawning of a new day of opportunity for the Church that would endure well beyond the time and place of its origins. The Church was being liberated from 'within' as it "not only lent its voice to the poor but sought out their voice and let it sound out within the churches" (Sobrino, 1979:290-291).

A new hope is slowly erupting on the margins of the Church the world over. Here, in Ireland, liberation is being felt on the periphery, outside the boundaries of old, as people discover new spiritual pathways to sustain them through the uncertainties of our time: "They may be disenchanted with the way they see Christianity being lived out around them, but they have not given up the search for a system of belief and spiritual practice which affirms and nourishes their own spiritual experiences" (Dorr, 2004:208). More and more people are struggling to withstand the torment of an economic storm that shows little sign of abating. The securities of the past are no longer guaranteed; many find themselves unable to meet repayments on house mortgages, established businesses are closing, austerity measures are starting to bite, and in the meantime up to 40,000 people leave our shores each year in pursuit of a better life. A new threshold is being crossed daily as families throughout the country know what it is like to be at the mercy of social forces over which they have little control. In the process, people have become more cognisant of the anomalies of a society that favours the privileged few at the expense of the weak and the powerless. Amid the tempest, people seek refuge and support. The Church cannot stand idly by and remain immune to the anguish of those most exposed to the ravages of today. The people are quietly but resolutely taking the lead in this regard. New movements of Church are slowly percolating to the surface: "Today, something more than the Church is required, something that is rooted in, and supported by, those informed and inspired members of a local community who are prepared to put time and energy into building a better future for its members" (Byrne, 2008:101).

Even as one model of Church declines, another grows; as one way of doing things collapses another takes on life. What is slowly evolving on the sidelines is not an alternative Church but a more accurate representation of what the Church was always intended to be. The energy and enthusiasm palpable in the many community organisations and ecological groups springing up around the country reflect a growing consciousness of the equilibrium that must be preserved between all strands in the web of life and a concern for the wellbeing of those who endure most when this balance is ruptured. Whilst these movements may not be explicitly religious in their motivation, they tap into a spiritual energy that might otherwise go unharnessed: "There is a real hunger for spirituality in our time. Many people who have become disillusioned with formal religions ... seek peace of mind, harmony with their neighbours, healing and reconciliation for wounded relationships, justice in society, and a sense of communion with nature" (Dorr, 2004:7). Ganiel reveals how "these people did not turn to the traditional organs of the institutional Church for help in growing their faith" but discovered in these 'extra-institutional spaces' a more authentic expression of spirituality that "they had not encountered in the Catholic parishes and schools which they had attended previously" (Ganiel, 2012:43). O'Brien's observations in *Seeds of a New Church* (1994) retain their relevance and significance two decades later: "As disillusionment grows with the institutionalisation of the church, some may give up on it but others search and struggle for other ways to be Christian community and to challenge the wider church to renew itself by forming communities, more real, more living and more relevant" (O' Brien, 1994:34).

Our Christian identity impels us outwards towards active community engagement rather than inwards towards a purely passive and introspective spiritual life. Rahner predicts in *Basic Communities* (1983) that the Church in the Western world will one day leave the deeply engrained ways of the past behind in favour of a more communal style of spiritual expression: "I suspect that the element of a fraternal, spiritual fellowship, of a communally lived spirituality, can play a greater part and be slowly but courageously acquired and developed" (Rahner, 1983:152). Christian communities that reach out to those who are over-burdened and downtrodden echo in their time and place the empathy and compassion Jesus had for those on the margins: "This community, then, is the Church of Jesus Christ whose mission in the world is to carry forward in history what Jesus did during his lifetime" (Haight, 1985:175). The preference of Christ was not to lecture, condemn or judge those who erred, but to sit alongside them, share a meal with them, listen to them and try to give hope and self-belief to those who felt excluded.

Christians today, just as 2,000 years ago, are called to "boldly take the initiative, go out to others, seek those who have fallen away, stand at the crossroads and welcome the outcast" (Pope Francis, 2013:20). The Christian community comes to life in its solidarity with those who suffer, in listening to the broken, in equipping the needy with the tools necessary to overcome their impoverishment, in simply making time for people amid the hardships and confusions of life: "Only in community can faith be lived in love. Only in community can faith be celebrated and deepened. Only in community can faith be lived in a life of fidelity to the Lord and solidarity with all men and women" (Gutiérrez, 1983:67).

This emerging dynamic of Church provides an antidote to the prevailing social ideologies that deny rather than promote all that is good in humanity. The Church, as 'contrast society', now becomes a place where the values of the Gospel are not compromised for other values no matter how appealing these values may appear. It is hard to resist the lure of the trappings of materialism and the ever revolving conveyor belt of digital advancements that have become the barometer of success in the Western world. The accessories on show date with an alacrity that defies the hype with which they were announced to the world. It is all too easy to get drawn into a whirlpool of competitiveness and become "caught in a never satisfied quest for achievement that ultimately produces a bottomless pit of anxiety ... seeking to get more, to have more, so as to control the future ... a route out of this morass is needed" (Social Justice Ireland, 2012:35). An increasingly consumerist world leaves many people struggling for meaning and contentment in life.

Small Christian communities are defined by their compassion for the oppressed, believing that in giving selflessly for others rather than accumulating for self that humanity comes to discover true happiness. Reaching out to those forgotten in the shadows of society helps us to unravel the vestiges of secularism and uncover what is of perennial value. We become attuned to a new frequency, something altogether different from the dictates of a culture that promises more than it can deliver: "Building a strong sense of community, a community that has the self-confidence to reach out and welcome into their midst the stranger, the immigrant and those on the margins ... is the direction in which we can seek to fill the vacuum created by the values that today's culture imposes on us" (McVerry, 2006:75).

Civilisation has reached an impasse in its movement through history. Individualism and technology have gone too far; the illusion of a better world that accentuates material gain over all other considerations is slowly evaporating. The sense of being alone and abandoned to a system that is indifferent to your plight is one that is applicable to the West just as it is to the developing world. In an ever more anonymous and anonymously guided society like ours today, people are searching for something new: "We are in need of a new paradigm for living together. Such a new paradigm will be based on better relations with the Earth, which will inaugurate a new social pact between peoples" (Boff, 2007:1-2). Times necessitate a more compassionate way for humanity to live together. Small Christian communities create the conditions that make this possible. The genesis of what is to come is already upon us: "A renaissance is coming. Soon there will be a multitude of communities founded on adoration and presence to the poor, linked to each other and to the great communities of the Church, which are themselves being renewed ... A new Church is indeed being born" (Vanier, 1979:59).

Communities Charged

with the Spirit

T he creative dynamism of Christian communities across Latin America in recent times contrasts distinctly with the somewhat jaded and impassive expressions of Church that many outside of the developing world have become accustomed to today. New levels of participation are encouraged in these communities that "prod the church to open itself to new interpretations, or challenge it to live out the spirit of the early Christian Church" (McGovern, 1989:223). The co-ordinator is the powerhouse of the community; organising liturgy, allocating responsibility to others in areas of education and service and mobilising all the members of the community to work towards their shared aspirations. Each ministry, in turn, has its own leader who acts in consultation with the co-ordinator to introduce varied initiatives that are not "predetermined by an attempt to preserve a pre-existing structure but are responses to needs as they arise" (Boff, 1985:119).

Leaders resist all forms of authoritarianism, preferring to achieve a consensus among the people for any of the projects to be undertaken by the community. The clerical monopoly of power yields to something more inclusive as the people become 'ecclesial subjects' in their own right: "In the base communities, almost entirely made up of lay people, one sees the true creation of an ecclesial reality ... lay people take the word in their own hands, create symbols and rites, and rebuild the Church with grassroot materials" (Boff, 1985:119).

The roles of leadership and coordination are shared and so power becomes a function of the community rather than of one single person. People with a background in education teach basic literacy skills to encourage individual members of their community to raise their own expectations in life. Others with a flair for organising campaigns and protests devise specific strategies aimed at tackling the oppressive conditions that their families have to contend with. Some with a natural propensity to care may help in visiting and comforting the sick. Those endowed with musical talent are invited to play an active part in the planning of liturgical events and to enrich their celebrations with songs and hymns that carry a particular resonance for their community. The Spirit is no longer hidden from the world but becomes perceptible in the incorrigible witness of the people. Those once silent have stepped in from the periphery and claimed their place in ways previously unimagined. All that once was is no more: "They do not want to hear people talking 'at' them about God; they want to experience God directly, to feel the Spirit moving in their hearts and guiding their lives. They want to experience community, to feel warm with people, to love and be loved, to celebrate. They want a spirituality which is earthy, of the body, but which at the same time finds an echo in their souls." (Dorr, 2004:7)

Christian Communities on the sidelines of the Church throughout the developing world have created the conditions for women to extend their sphere of influence beyond the home and bring their own transformative energies to bear on the wider social arena. The stoic resolve of multitudes of women to effect change is helping them to shape society rather than be shaped by society, and, in the process, break free from the old cultural assumptions of the past: "Women's power of transformation still encounters obstacles when it comes to the manifestation of all its potential, but it is beginning to gain its own space ... They learn that liberation of the marginalized is a daily victory, and a dynamic, creative process initiated by themselves" (Tepedino and Ribeiro Brandão, 1993:221-222) Whilst many women participate assiduously in everything from catechesis to social outreach as co-ordinators in their communities, some still find that their leadership is limited within the constraints of the overarching patriarchal structure of Church "which is hierarchical and male ... a model of the oppressive man-woman relationship" (Ferro, 1981:28). Ferro anticipates a time when women at the 'base' are elevated to positions where they can have a greater say in the governance of the Church and be empowered with the skills and education necessary to exert real influence: "This is urgently needed. Women should also be trained to undertake the work of educating, systematizing, and leading" (Ferro, 1981:36).

Pastoral agents play a pivotal role in the life of these grassroots Christian communities in Latin America. They act as an essential lifeline between the institution and the people and provide each community with the support and training needed to sustain it as it evolves. The bishops organise workshops for their pastoral agents in everything from liturgical celebration to land rights and the pastoral agents, in turn, meet with the co-ordinators in their area to provide them with the resources necessary to implement worthwhile projects in their communities. A new alliance between the institution and the people is forged. Pastoral agents secure the indissoluble bond between the two. The margins now become central to the task of Church. Yet, the support these communities receive from the hierarchy has waned significantly since their inception. Over recent decades, bishops who once championed the rights of the people so selflessly were replaced as part of an intentional strategy by Rome to quell the surge in momentum at the grassroots and restore order. This vital tie between the institution and the people weakened and the network of support all but disappeared. Boff explains that the only real tension that exists is "between a Church that has opted for the people, for the poor and their liberation, and other groups in that same Church ... who persist in keeping to the strictly sacramental and devotional character of faith" (Boff, 1985:126). Pope Francis, in marked contrast to some of his predecessors, is unequivocal in his support of these communities and has placed increased emphasis on their potential to "bring a new evangelising fervour and a new capacity for dialogue with the world whereby the Church is renewed" (Pope Francis, 2013:23). It is time to re-visit old pathways in the search for new horizons.

Small Christian communities venture beyond the alienating structures of the past into new frontiers: "These core communities and core groups are expected to give new life to the congregations of the established church and at the same time to strike out new paths linking the church to society as a whole" (Moltmann, 1977:332). Gemma Peelo and Delores Connell were members of a leadership team of co-ordinators in the 'Crumlin Small Christian Community', Dublin during the 1990s. Connell explains how three people were elected each year to act as "a smaller community within the community" to plan meetings and to prioritise whatever issues or topics were pertinent to the group at any given time. At least one member of the leadership team would continue into the next term to ensure that there was a natural succession from one team to the next. Connell acclaims the achievement of each new team of leaders in steering the community along a path that reflected the views and convictions of the entire community: "Leadership is not about imposing an agenda on others without dialogue or consultation but involves listening to the opinions of others, even the dissenting voice, so that everyone has a say in determining the course of action that leads on from the discussion." Peelo outlines how each member of the team opted to take on responsibilities most suited to their distinctive abilities; one organised guest speakers on issues of social justice that the team felt were important to the community, another explored new practices in the area of spirituality that she could then bring to the community and the third co-ordinated the programme of Gospel reflection so that everyone in the community had the opportunity to lead the meeting at some point over the year: "Our spiritual journey and our social conscience led us to the same starting point. We listened to our inner voice and acted accordingly. Together, as one community, we set about working towards specific goals that helped us to make a difference to the lives of others."

The Church must be concerned with every dimension of life and not limited to some exclusive spiritual or religious sphere. If the institution retreats from history, it effectively severs its ties with the recurring presence of the Spirit in the world. People at the grassroots see themselves as being constantly on the road rather than having already reached their destiny. Each defining moment on the journey has its own importance and the Spirit is what sustains them along the way: "They are a community of the faithful in which the Risen Christ is present" (Boff, 1985:126). The people share in the movement of the Spirit without mediation and actualise its liberating power in their response to the religious, social and political needs of their community: "They are no longer just parishioners in a parish; they have their own ecclesiological value; they are recreating the Church of God" (Boff, 1985:126). Ministries in such diverse spheres as catechetical instruction or liturgical celebration exist alongside ministries in areas of social justice allowing the all-pervading presence of the Spirit to intervene in the life of the community in real and tangible ways. Christian ministry is being re-defined on a daily basis in the unwavering resolve of the people to overcome the fatalism of old and become protagonists in their own history: "At this point Christian ministry makes a choice. Christian faith and love impels an analysis of such situations from the point of view of the victims of society, and its ministry should be dedicated to a change that engenders equality" (Haight, 1985:231).

The vision of Church emanating from Latin America is making its presence felt in over 200,000 communities throughout the world. These communities are not isolated movements, totally detached from each other, but exist as interrelated parts in a universal network of communities that are re-shaping the dynamic of Church in the world today: "Small Christian communities, though having their own relative autonomy, ought to be open to one another and can combine in a parish or wherever so as to form a communion of communities" (O'Halloran, 2010:17). In his book, *Living Cells: Vision and Practicalities of Small Christian Communities and Groups* (2010), O'Halloran reveals how the ongoing activity Spirit is the vital strand that is woven seamlessly through these communities, binding them together into one unified movement to define the landscape of the new Church: "We must pray fervently for these small communities, this nascent church, which is such a splendid example of the Holy Spirit working in the people of God" (O'Halloran, 2010:192). O'Halloran recalls how the Greeks in the early Church used the word 'choreuein' (dance) to capture how the creative vibrancy that exists between each of the persons of the Trinity cannot be contained within the past but continues to make its presence felt through history. The choreography that animates the multitude of small Christian communities around the world is very much sealed by the same life force that unites the Father, Son and the Holy Spirit. As a consequence, the activity of the Spirit is never exhausted. It finds expression in each new age in places where God's love is keenly felt: "As a corollary of being motivated by the Trinity, the communities have a refined sense of being permeated by the love of God" (O'Halloran, 2010:55).

Claire Cassells and Bridie Clancy have been actively involved in their 'Leixlip Parish Cell Community' and reveal how their cell remains autonomous yet connected to a wider movement of cell communities that has now 'multiplied' to fourteen cells in their parish and to over 150 cells throughout Ireland. Each parish cell meets weekly in groups of 8–10 people in a home of one of the members and provides a setting where people come together to reflect on their experiences in light of the inspiration they draw from the Gospel. The institutional Church plays a decisive role in overseeing the development of each cell community, recording a weekly 'teaching' to guide each cell in their spiritual discernment and organising a diocesan gathering of cells every three months to exchange ideas and resources. Clancy explains how the identity of each community revolves around "the oikos philosophy of evangelisation" which is grounded on the conviction that "everyday relationships that are nurtured in a home or 'oikos' environment, and the ongoing interactions that arise from these relationships, are extremely significant in the process of passing on the faith." Cassells reveals how each cell provides a reflective space for the development of a deeper faith and the combined spiritual energies of the network of cells in their locality breathe fresh life into their wider parish community: "The institution and the parish cell communities co-exist. They need each other to survive. Yet, the institution recedes into the background and something more meaningful and more representative of the people takes its place. The seeds of change have taken root."

The Church as we know it is being re-invented on the fringes. The emergence of smaller, more intimate faith communities creates a platform for people to take ownership of their own faith development and become attuned to the deeper, spiritual realm at the core of their existence: "Ordinary Christian people must reclaim and revalue their own experience, affirm the loving and active presence of the Holy Spirit in their own story, and then articulate their story as a paragraph in the story of God" (Byrne, 2008:94). Small Christian communities are not mere appendages to the Church that carry little significance in the universal scheme of things but are integral to the process of re-aligning the Church with its source in the immediacy of each new time and place: "So we can know God through other people, for when we experience love from our fellow human beings, we are experiencing God ... The best road towards knowing God is through living community" (O'Halloran, 2010:27).

Many of these communities owe their origins to the creative vision of people who have discovered in the unique witness of people on the margins of society those very qualities needed to give renewed hope to the Church's mission in the world at this time. The Church cannot stand still. The reins of its destiny rest in the hands of its people: "The Church must look for them and carry them within itself. It must listen to them and let itself be transformed by them" (Wresinski, 2002:38-39).

The Liberating Power
of the Gospel

The Gospel is the spiritual compass that gives direction to the activities of small Christian communities around the world today. The people come together once or twice a week in small clusters of fifteen to twenty families to hear the Word and reflect on its significance in their lives: "An interesting phenomenon of our times is that the Bible is to be found back in the hands of the laity. It is no longer the sole preserve of the cleric or the scholar. This is a wholesome development because it was written by ordinary people for ordinary people in the first place" (O'Halloran, 2010:41). The Christian story is etched indelibly into the psyche of small Christian communities and provides them with a lens for looking at life and ascertaining what is of lasting importance.

The Word is present amid the difficulties and the joys of everyday and filters out into all facets of life within the community: "The word of God is not just the Bible. The word of God is within reality and it can be discovered there with the help of the Bible" (Mesters, 1981:122). The Gospel speaks to people within the context of their own suffering and strengthens their resolve to persevere in the face of persecution: We now "have a community of people meeting around the Bible who inject concrete reality and their own situation into the discussion. Their struggle as a people enters the picture" (Mesters, 1981:199).

The Gospel becomes the point of reference for these communities. The reading of the Gospel passage is not an end in itself but a prelude to a course of action that unveils its significance to the world. The truths contained within the chosen lines now become authenticated by the lived response to these truths. Christian praxis hinges on this unique interplay between reflection and action. The meaning of the Word is discovered in the action and the ensuing reflection on the Word can shape and influence the course of subsequent action. The heightened levels of discernment that flow from this cyclical dynamic act as a stimulus for change in the wider social arena: "A 'praxis situation' is one in which theory and practice are not separable. Each continually influences, and is influenced by, the other; as the mutual interchange goes on, they are not only constantly transforming one another, but are transforming the overall situation as well" (McAfee Brown, 1990:65).

The Gospel is always confronted with life and the response to the Word follows its own distinctive course in each community. If members of the community are suffering from illness, a team of carers will make sure the needs of these people and their families are met. If a member is imprisoned for advocating action in support of the land rights or improved social conditions for their community, the family of that member will be supported by the community for the duration of his/her time away: "The basis of these communities is the word of God that is heard and re-read within the context of their real problems; they are held together by their faith, their communitarian projects, their helping one another, and their celebrations" (Boff, 1985:121).

The interpretation ascribed to the Gospel in small Christian communities bears the stamp of humanity of a curious people. The community gravitates towards the Word and access to its hallowed truths is reached through a communal, shared reading rather than an atomised or individualistic study. The Gospel is incomplete and the finishing lines are inscribed in the human story unique to each person who reads it: "If our pilgrimage is to unfold the vision rather than merely repeat the past, then the present cannot passively inherit and repeat the story. We must appropriate the story critically within the present experience, reclaim it, add to it with our own creative word and in that sense change it" (Groome, 1980:194). This dialectic between the Word and the world creates an opening for people to bring their pain, their joys, their brokenness and their hopes to the Gospel and to be enlightened by the timeless significance of all they discover.

The message implicit in the Word is not parachuted down from a mystical world beyond all that we know but is unearthed from the reservoir of experience that we bring to the Word: "Such dialogues between experience and faith frequently create and clarify meanings and reshape lives, and they provide a supportive community during the struggle for meaning and direction. If not for small Christian communities, many persons would have no place to talk about their faith and their relationships in the presence of others who care" (O'Halloran, 2010:190).

Yvonne Daly and Mary McQuaide have been members of 'The Fig Tree Group' in Fatima Mansions for thirty years now and they provide a unique perspective on the centrality of the Gospel in the life of a small Christian community. McQuaide captures how their community draws them into the fathomless depths of their own being to a place where they come to know Jesus as a friend and guide: "My time with 'The Fig Tree' gives me the space to pray with others in community. I feel that I find Jesus in every page. He speaks to me in the silence, in the reflections of others and in the solidarity we experience as a group. We are no longer alone and the Gospel story becomes part of our lives in a special way." Daly clarifies how the Gospel is woven into the pattern of their meetings in a simple yet purposeful manner. A Gospel passage is chosen by a member of their group in advance of their meeting and becomes a focal point for the discussions that unfold over the course of the meeting. They are then invited to identify a word or phrase from the chosen passage and to reflect on how it carries a particular relevance for them. The exploration of a Gospel passage never follows a prescribed and preordained route but very much reflects the rich and varied responses of each person to the passage. Daly reflects on how the inherent trust between all members of the group has been sealed over years of friendship and sharing and has given her confidence in the intrinsic worth of her own beliefs: "Years ago the Bible was above my head. I now read a piece and understand it. People listen to me, hear what I'm saying and understand where my thoughts are coming from. We learn from each other and the Gospel takes on a whole new meaning in our lives."

There is an acceptance in these small Christian communities that any attempt to promote the spiritual in a way that does not issue a corresponding action is spurious and vacant. These communities are reflective but don't simply luxuriate in reflection. Their antennae are always facing outward, deciphering ways of making the kingdom real and not illusory. The prevalence of injustice and persecution in our world is a stark reminder that as long as there is suffering in the world the kingdom has not yet arrived. In his book *The Meaning is in the Shadows* (2003), McVerry widens the domain in which the kingdom is rolled out in history to encompass the multiplicity of ways in which all people of goodwill, irrespective of their faith, build a better world: "We can all therefore become involved in building the Kingdom. Wherever we are living, whatever we are working at, there we can help to build the Kingdom" (McVerry, 2003:37). The more humanity engages in small, unheralded projects that promote all that is good, the more each community of faith can signify the arrival of the Kingdom in the cut and thrust of their history: "When I ask, then, where do we find the Kingdom growing here on earth, we look, not for some earth shattering event, but for small projects that no-one knows about, which are trying to improve the quality of life for those who are on the margins. It is the small little efforts, in unheard-of housing estates or isolated rural communities, which are the typical signs of the Kingdom of God" (McVerry, 2003:37).

Small Christian communities are places where the presence of the kingdom of justice and peace is manifested visibly and effectively through the humanity of the people. These communities create the conditions necessary for the kingdom to find its roots in the indigenous soil of each new age: "This spirituality has a faith that sees the Kingdom of God in the little bits and pieces of history where people are being served and cared for by other people" (Haight, 1985:256). God has entrusted humanity with a project to be built, developed and brought to its completion in each new time and place: "This world is the arena where God's ultimate plan for creation unfolds. The Kingdom of God happens here, in the midst of our human affairs. It is meant for this world here and now, although its future fulfillment is still to come" (Fuellenbach, 1995:201). The kingdom is not a 'fait accompli'; it is something that is evolving, growing and moving closer to its accomplishment in history. The 'eschatology' of the kingdom, this oscillation between 'what is now' and 'what is yet to come', compels each community to see in the present a movement towards something that has not yet been fully realised. The challenge is to narrow the chasm between the two: "It does so by doing for men and women here and now, in new situations ... what Jesus did in his time: raising them up for the coming Kingdom of God, caring for the poor and outcast ... serving all men and women in solidarity" (Schillebeeckx, 1990:157).

Theological inquiry cannot side-step the adversities of today in favour of the promise of what is to come in the future: "The mere postulate of another world or an after-life by itself may undermine the meaning of the actual history of this world" (Haight, 1985:134). The corollary of this is clear and its significance cannot be understated; we do not discover meaning by becoming subsumed in a mysterious realm beyond the parameters of this world but create meaning in the here and now: "But the Christian is one who is convinced that he or she is called to create or make meaning within history by the use of his or her own freedom" (Haight, 1985:247).

God's Word and hints of transcendence often lie concealed behind the veil of obdurate social forces that deny people their most basic needs. Our abhorrence at the scale and intensity of suffering in the world today compel us to absorb the often opaque world of scriptural reflection into the realm of the everyday so that it becomes a vehicle of liberation for all people: "The gospel is not something that comes from outside, culturally. It is a seed which sprouts from the ground of their suffering and oppressed lives and which breaks the hardness of that ground precisely because it is rooted therein" (Barreiro, 1982:30). The poor cannot be excluded from this process but must be encouraged to bring their innate sensitivities and wisdom to bear on all efforts to make the Word meaningful and intelligible in the world today: "What other path is there for a theology? We have to draw our reflection, as well as our practice, from the experience of the poorest people, not from an idea that we have of their existence but from the reality of their daily lives" (Wresinski, 2002:161).

The spiritual orientation of the small Christian community leans towards the kingdom and becomes a springboard for social action. 'St. Angela's Peace and Justice Group' epitomises how each small Christian community can awaken a new social consciousness of the needs of the silenced and the forgotten in situations of great persecution today. Over the last few decades, several generations of students campaigned vociferously to heighten awareness of injustice and place a spotlight on the suffering of people whose story often goes untold. During the first half of the academic year, the students met at lunchtime and organised themselves into smaller working groups on issues ranging from the problem of homelessness in cities around Ireland to the plight of people under military rule in Burma. Each group researched their chosen topics, identified guest speakers, worked on artistic displays and then presented their findings during a 'Peace and Justice Week' in the school in March. Sinéad Fitzpatrick, the student co-ordinator in 1998, reveals how her time in the 'Peace and Justice Group' made a lasting impression on her and inspired her to believe in her capacity to effect change: "Whether it was Nobel laureates like John Hume or Bishop Carlos Belo or local people who worked tirelessly to help others, the sincerity of their story left a deep imprint." Fitzpatrick recalls John Pilger's account of the massacre of hundreds of young students at the 'Santa Cruz Cemetery' in East Timor at the hands of the Indonesian armed troops: "There was a numbing silence as his words and accompanying film footage brought us face to face with the horror of Santa Cruz. We realised that their fate could well have been ours. The screams of the East Timorese students shook us out of our indifference. There was no turning back. The silenced need people to speak and act on their behalf." The call to be a voice for the voiceless is one that ignites something deep within. It simply cannot be ignored.

God's kingdom is mediated through community, through the bonds of solidarity and friendship that are moulded over time as Christians come together to reflect on the Gospel and translate its significance in ways that give hope to those most burdened in their midst: "The church is most obviously discernible in small Christian communities; in practice it is these that are at the cutting edge of testimony and action" (O'Halloran, 2010:35). The smallest instances of love, compassion, concern for someone in need of care or enlightenment has the power to impact on their lives. The minscule and apparently insignificant can be profound and trigger a process of transformation within the individual that seeps out into the world where this new found freedom is exercised. In the deed the Word becomes truth, not only for others, but for ourselves as well: "God's word is enfleshed in this place and does not return to God empty handed" (Byrne, 2008:33). Love translates the kingdom that is to come into the possibilities of today. Reflection on the Word sets in motion a chain reaction that knows no bounds: "We may be sure that none of our acts of love will be lost, nor any of our acts of sincere concern for others. No single act of love for God will be lost, no generous effort is meaningless, no painful endurance is wasted. All of these encircle our world like a vital force" (Pope Francis, 2013:136).

The Prophetic Voice
of the Church

Small Christian communities provide the catalyst for people in situations of great social and political upheaval to find their own prophetic voice and to work resolutely to free themselves from the demoralising grip of social inequality. In these communities, the Church opts decisively for those on the margins of society and supports them in their efforts to overcome the abject poverty that has been inflicted on them by the dominant classes: "The Church is no longer a Church simply for the poor and the unprotected. Now it is a Church made up of the poor and unprotected" (Boff, 1989:203).

The faith of the community is not a fatalistic resignation to all that appears unchanging but a defiant call that stirs people to engage in the task of shaping their own destinies and transforming all that they can no longer tolerate in their surrounds. Projects are identified in basic health care, literacy programmes are introduced and local co-operatives are formed securing the fundamental rights of all not just the privileged elite. A genuine conversion process is happening at the grassroots as bishops and priests challenge the people to see beyond the desolation of their present existence and aspire towards more equitable social conditions for their communities. The journey of the Church through history is beginning to resemble its humble origins: "The future of the institutional Church lies in this small seed that is the new Church growing in the fields of the poor and powerless" (Boff, 1985:63).

The voice of a prophetic people never surrenders to the dehumanising dictates of an unequal world. Many multi-national companies have their base in Latin America and operate to the persistent cadence of an economic crusade that reaps what it can from the natural resources of the land with minimal interest in the wage entitlements of their employees or in the ecological wasteland they leave in their wake. Cheap labour in impoverished conditions means greater profit. Will World Cup 2014 or Olympics 2016 impact positively on the lives of the poor in favellas around Brazil? The ruling elite harvest rich reward whilst the powerless are heaved from the streets with considerable disdain so that their protests are removed from the glare of a watching world. A resurgent people will not lie down and die. They will not be intimidated by the merciless forces that seek to crush their rights and stifle their spirit. Yet, sport can reconcile differences and break down historic divides. Nelson Mandela's wearing of the South African jersey in the Rugby World Cup final of 1995 unified a nation in an instant. The South African people, black and white, rejoiced in shared jubilation at a triumph that went beyond the boundaries of sport. History can produce timeless moments that have the capacity to shape the course of what is to come. The poor have not got time on their hands. The future they aspire towards cannot be reached alone.

A Church that stands adrift from the afflictions of its people and somewhat muted in the face of injustice is complicit in imprisoning those it claims to serve within an endless spiral of hardship and persecution. To remain silent in the face of injustice is to endorse the dominant ideology that holds it together and to encourage a passive acceptance of this ideology. Gutiérrez argues that just as the Church must offer "a radical critique of the present order ... the Church must also criticise itself as an integral part of this order" (Gutiérrez, 1988:240). When the Church speaks out, it announces the good news of the kingdom to the poor and denounces what is in flagrant contradiction to it. The Church does not exist to propagate the existing societal norms but "to evoke an alternative community that knows it is about different things in different ways" (Brueggemann, 1982:110-111). This necessitates a clear and unambiguous rebuke of the oppressive forces that enslave the poor and a willingness to walk alongside them in their tenacious strides towards freedom. The prophetic voice carries with it real responsibility: "Each individual Christian and every community is called to be an instrument of God for the liberation and promotion of the poor, and for enabling them to be fully a part of society" (Pope Francis, 2013:98).

To step aside and abdicate our responsibility to decry the remorseless exploitation of our fellow human beings would mean that this moment in history would reach its "aporia ... the point at which there really seems to be no way through, namely, at the point of the powerlessness of love against injustice" (Sobrino, 1985:34-35). Knowing that the transference of barely 4% of the 225 greatest fortunes in the world would be sufficient to provide food, water, health and education to the whole of humanity, why is this tolerated? Is there not something gravely amiss in a world where the market value of the panel of a top Premier League or La Liga football team might well equal a major proportion of a black African nation's annual budget?

Part of the macro blasphemy of our time is the reality that 2.5 billion people survive on Earth on less than two euros a day and 25,000 persons die of hunger every day. We who buy into the trappings of consumerism are numbed by our submission to the world view of those who profit from our acceptance. It is not simply unjust, but disturbingly wrong, that a Salvadoran woman in a sweat-shop earns twenty-nine cents for each shirt that the multinational Nike sells to the NBA for forty-five dollars. The poor live ensnared in a web of oppression spun by the rich in their voracious pursuit of the vestiges of success. As long as this reality is maintained as absolute and untouchable "human beings will be classified according to their ability to produce wealth, their right to possess and enjoy wealth will prolong and even increase human oppression, and most certainly it will widen the distance between the haves and the have-nots" (Sobrino, 2008:39).

Society often denies the poor the inalienable right to self-expression, yet, the more they are empowered to speak, the more likely they are to make their voice heard in the world. At the grassroots of the Church across the developing world, people regularly plan demonstrations to resist land takeovers or organise protest marches to object to the adverse social conditions that they are subjected to. What is transpiring is a new awakening among people once powerless in society as they "develop a consciousness of their oppressed situation, organize themselves, and take steps that will lead to a society that is less dependent and less subject to injustices" (Boff, 1985:7-8). With the support and guidance of pastoral agents, priests and bishops in the wider Church community, the people participate in literacy programmes and begin to reflect critically on the problem-posing situations that they encounter in their daily lives. The impetus for change arises from within the community and reverberates outwards. Freire's word for this process, *conscientization*, has become a symbol of the possibility of dignity and power being restored to the poor, as they are 'conscientized' to their actual situation, understand it anew and opt to change it: "Problem-posing education bases itself on creativity and stimulates true reflection and action upon reality, thereby responding to the vocation of men (and women) as beings who are authentic only when engaged in inquiry and creative transformation" (Freire, 1970:56). A new humanity is being moulded among an assertive people intent on change: "Now the gospel would be taken over by the poor and used by them for the purpose for which it was written" (Boff, 1989:13).

The identity of each community is very much moulded by the distinctive prophetic qualities of its leaders. These men and women have the vision to transcend the overwhelming negativity and sense of foreboding that exists in times of crisis and become bearers of real hope in their community: "But a group that envisages a goal and truly wishes to attain it must still be encouraged to persevere amid the difficulties that are encountered in reaching the goal. A true leader provides such encouragement by instilling in the group some of his/her own hope" (Cooke, 1976:208). The prophet has the vision to anticipate in the present the channel through which the community must pass if they are to reach their shared destiny. Hope now becomes the 'driving force' of the community and draws their people into "the very heart of history, in the midst of a single process of liberation which leads that history to its fulfilment in the definitive encounter with God" (Gutiérrez, 1988:223-224).

The hope of the community triumphs in those very situations that threaten its existence. Their faith sustains them through the storm: "The characteristic darkness of faith ... is mediated by the black darkness of hope" (Sobrino, 1984:155). The utopian vision that drives these communities onwards is not an escape from the oppressive realities of today but rather a stimulus for the transformation of these realities so that they no longer exist. The people know that this journey is not made on their own: "Day by day Jesus generates in them the hope that liberation and the reign of God will come – despite the enormous obstacles in its way" (Sobrino, 1985:173-174).

The theologians of liberation have been greatly influenced by the sixteenth century theologian Bartolome de Las Casas and recognise in his empathy with the plight of the indigenous Indians in the Latin America a more prophetic way of giving witness to the Gospel. The more Las Casas observed the suffering and persecution inflicted on the native Indian population, the more he distanced himself from the European mindset that tolerated such destruction and devastation. Las Casas and his fellow evangelisers began to interpret life from the standpoint of those most exposed to the tyranny and plundering of the adventurers and: "... gradually divested themselves of their spontaneous sense of superiority and sought to move to the viewpoint of the dispossessed. This effort enabled them to read history in a different way and to understand the meaning of the swift and violent events of those years from the other side of that history" (Gutiérrez in Nickoloff, 1996:281). Las Casas deviated from the norm, from what was sanctioned from authority. His source became the gospels and his inspiration came from the recipients of the Christian message. When the Church has the suffering of its people as its starting point as Las Casas did, it too becomes susceptible to the presence of Christ in their brokenness and pain: "He saw in the Indian, in this "other," this one-different-from-the-Westerner, the poor one of the gospel, and ultimately Christ himself" (Gutierrez in Nickoloff, 1996:282). It is here in the unique testimony of its people that the Church discovers its own prophetic voice.

Communities with a prophetic radar reflect a counter movement to the orientations of a society that bind people to a set of unremitting circumstances from which there can appear no way out. The *Shaping Ireland's Future* Report (2012) commissioned by Social Justice Ireland highlights the growing disparity between rich and poor in Irish society and reveals that a widening number of people fall into the poverty net in Ireland today: "Of all the children (under 18 years of age) in Ireland,

19.5% live in poverty – more than 200,000 children. The scale of this statistic, which has increased in recent years, is alarming. Given that our children are our future, this situation is not acceptable" (Social Justice Ireland, 2012:45).

Viewed from the underworld, life takes on a new perspective. People in areas of dire destitution are conditioned to think and act in a particular way and are drawn in to a cycle of poverty from which there is little hope of escape. Violence, crime, gangland killings and drug abuse all contribute to a deeply sinister and troubling negation of all that is good in humanity. Yet, in most cases, a life of crime or drug addiction is predetermined for the children from the time they are born. Not all who relinquish their grip on a dignified existence merit the derisory glance that is cast in their direction. Many on the outside shield themselves from unpalatable truths and remain hostage to a world they do not fully understand: "The more we have to protect, the stronger the tendency to insulate ourselves from those on the margins whom we may perceive as a threat to our security" (McVerry, 2008:24).

Small Christian communities have become synonymous with a radical option for the most alienated in society. The prophetic word can never be caged in; it pre-empts a course of action that embodies its significance in the world. Human compassion anchors the prophetic vision in the challenges of today. Real solidarity with the poor is forged not through occasional acts of mercy from the sidelines of their existence but by sharing their burdens to some degree and experiencing their sense of being powerless and on the margins: "Commitment to the poor means entering into their universe and living in it. It means not going into this world for a few hours in order to bear witness to the gospel, but rather emerging from it each morning to proclaim the good news to every human being" (Gutiérrez, 1986:10).

Françoise Barbier from 'ATD Fourth World' insists that compassion for the downtrodden in society does not happen effortlessly but requires a selfless and deliberate act of letting go of all that once defined us. Their movement is founded on the premise that human misery recedes wherever people unite to eradicate it. Barbier explains how they have covered mud floors, installed water and electricity, opened centres of learning, built kindergartens and family centres in their endeavour to give of their time and energies to alleviate the suffering of people who are stripped bare of their most basic rights. Barbier alludes to the message engraved on the stone dedicated to their founder, Joseph Wresinski, at the 'Plaza of Liberties and Human Rights' in Paris, to underline the importance of finding the time to listen to the story of those who remain voiceless in the world and encourage them in their efforts to shape their own history: "The world will change one day because we will have listened to the children of the poorest, and because these children will take their destiny in hand." Those who empower will themselves be empowered by all they experience among the poor.

A prophetic Church can reveal its face to the world in a multiplicity of ways. What we are witnessing on the margins is the emergence of social justice movements with a spiritual emphasis that create a space where communal reflection becomes possible. Resignation slowly but defiantly yields to a new hope as people in places where economic resources are scarce become protagonists in their own history. Their collective voice rises as one to transform the landscape of their impoverishment.

Gemma McKenna recalls how both she and Ciaran Earley, co-founders of 'Partners in Faith', met with representatives from many economically poor communities around Dublin in the late 1980s and conducted a series of workshops aimed at helping them to realise that they have resources within themselves to bring about real social transformation: "The workshops sought to stimulate a new positivity in the participants that would spill back into their communities and create openings for people to come together to reflect, to pray and to support each other through the difficulties and hardships that they experienced." When marginalised groups are encouraged to speak and act on their own behalf and have their experiences recognised, it affirms their identity and their worth as a people. Their discussions together open the door to a new style of social engagement. The root causes of poverty, once exposed, can be targeted with precision and purpose. McKenna reveals how some participants returned to their communities and rallied neighbours and friends to take a stand against crime; some highlighted the ravages of drug addiction and organised protests against traffickers in their locality; some campaigned vociferously to secure funding for libraries, adult education centres, leisure amenities and play areas for their children. McKenna emphasises the need for facilitators of these workshops to "hold back and only intervene if it encourages disadvantaged people themselves to articulate their own experience and to devise their own strategy of realistic action."

The prophetic voice of the Church champions the needs and rights of those silenced in society and testifies to the perennial truth that the spirituality of any Christian community "should not isolate or separate human beings from the world and other human beings but rather bind them to a common human existence in solidarity with others in the world" (Haight, 1985:240). Pope Francis is acutely aware of the difficulties faced by many people the world over today: "The hearts of many people are gripped by fear and desperation, even in the so-called rich countries ... It is a struggle to live and, often, to live with precious little dignity" (Pope Francis, 2013:35). Yet, no matter how interminable their suffering is, no matter how trapped they are in wretched social conditions, the poor possess reserves of decency and tenderness that remain resolute and undiminished. Their capacity to share moments of joy and laughter even in the face of immense suffering gives testimony to the resilience of their spirit. What is given is returned in abundance: "Now the road is open to a new incarnation of the gospel in a still-unreached continent, the continent of the poor. And a new kind of organization can spring up in the Church, an organization that is more popular, more shared, more closely connected with the cause of justice and a life worth living" (Boff, 1989:17).

Communities that
Dance to a New Rhythm

S mall Christian communities are energised by the natural ebullience of their people and their uplifting sense that God is close at hand. These communities do not wallow in despair at what appears insurmountable but instead look forward in the unwavering hope that they will one day wade through the waters of adversity and leave the exile of their past behind.

The Good News is not simply proclaimed; it is celebrated as a living presence in their history that leads them onwards towards freedom: "A people that knows how to celebrate is a people with hope. They are no longer a wholly oppressed people but a people who march toward their liberation" (Boff, 1985:130).

The worship of the faith community consolidates this closeness to God. They rejoice to the tune of their popular hymns and give thanks for all that God has done for them through their specially composed songs. Their prayers of petition are startling in the very concrete nature of their appeals and their creative use of drama and mime brings a striking realism to the ongoing revelation of the Word in their midst. When the community prays, it recalls their problems and hardships as well as their victories and successes and places them into the hands of a caring God: "It happens in a special way when the community comes together for prayer: prayers of petition or gratuitous praise, moments of talk and silence, and rituals of gesture and song. These are the moments when the people consciously meet their God, take repose in God, enjoy God's presence, and share the food and drink they need to keep moving on in hope" (Muñoz, 1981:156).

Religious expression at the grassroots assumes the culture of the people, their way of life, their joviality and their natural susceptibility to the sacred in the bits and pieces of their everyday lives. Across Latin America, the popular devotion of the people overflows from one community to the next as a series of melodic movements within the wider symphony of Church. Every community 'adopts' their own saints and applies their distinctive colour and pageantry to the processions and feast days that are intrinsic to their identity as a community.

Ferro reveals how communities at the 'base' of the Church identify ways of 'systematizing' their individual and collective experience of God: "There is a plethora of pamphlets, bulletins, songs, poetic pieces, and plays ... They bring together the living experience of the community, work it up, and then return it to the community" (Ferro, 1981:32). Liturgy is never purely ceremonial; it rises from the unbroken spirit of a believing people who live in the knowledge that they are not alone: "The poor suffer, yes; but they do not sorrow. To live with joy, to be glad to be alive, is to live with ultimate meaning – with the ability to be grateful and to celebrate, the ability to be for others and be with others"(Sobrino, 1993:251-252). These sacred gatherings drift almost unknowingly towards Mary, mother of the poor, who becomes a vivifying symbol of God's enduring love for the oppressed: "She becomes once more the simple woman, the woman of the people, the mother of Jesus the carpenter's son, in solidarity with her folk and with the hopes of her people, handmaid of that Lord who topples the mighty from their thrones and exalts the humble, who fills the poor with good things and sends the rich empty away" (Magaña, 1993:188).

God's love is the creative life force that surges through the activity of the Church in grassroots communities around the world today. In *We Drink from our own Wells* (2005), Gutiérrez reveals how God's grace surfaces at defining moments in life to rouse people to uncover a deeper, mystical dimension to their human existence: "At the root of every spirituality there is a particular experience that is had by concrete persons living at a particular time" (Gutiérrez, 2005:37). Life has its own spiritual undercurrents that each person can retrieve when they delve into the wellspring of their own experiences. The identity of each community, in turn, is often defined by personal or collective experiences of pain or joy of the community, "intense moments of encounter with the Lord" (Gutiérrez, 2005:42), that forge a permanent seal between the community and God.

These communities understand that access to this realm of mystery is not the exclusive privilege of mystics and spiritual leaders but is available to all: "There is the mysticism of everyday life, the discovery of God in all things ... Let us seek the specific experiences in which something like that happens to us" (Rahner, 1979:22). The faith of the people does not blind them to the harsher, less palatable realities of life but opens their eyes to the life-giving power of God's grace carrying them through their hour of persecution. The people intuitively grasp life's paradox; suffering is the gateway to truth, the path into the unknown. Their questions and their faith are intertwined; they proceed together: "God's dwelling in history is not simple and obvious, so that it may be found quickly, directly, and unmistakably. God is present in human history with its tensions, successes, and conflicts, but finding God requires a search" (Gutiérrez, 1991:80).

The very concrete expressions of service and love that are integral to the life of these communities make their joyous celebrations all the more authentic. God's grace is not ineffectual. It does not remain on the purely spiritual level, remote from this earthly history. Its effects are perceptible in "the continuum of human action" that translates the ideals of truth, love and justice into the concrete realities that are part of the fabric of each community (Comblin, 1993:212). The recipients of God's gift of grace have the responsibility to contribute to the outpouring of this grace among those most in need among them: "At the centre of our faith is the fact that God has loved us first, and that a response to that love, a love for our brothers and sisters, has its life from, and is imbued with the power of, being loved by God" (Sobrino, 1993:248). 'Filiation' now becomes the specific character of God's saving grace as "the Father's love ... makes us his daughters and sons ... transforms us, making us more fully human, more fully brothers and sisters to all" (Gutiérrez, 1983:67). When we embrace the struggles of our brothers and sisters as our own, we unveil the mystery of God's love in the world. Bethlehem is re-visited wherever people make time for the anonymous and insignificant ones of history: "Every person who is poor and forgotten is, like Bethlehem, unimportant, but from this person the Lord comes to us ... When we serve the poor we serve the Christ in whom we believe; when we are in solidarity with the neediest we discern the lowly reality of the son of man" (Gutiérrez, 1991:88).

Small Christian communities must become places where the unyielding spirit of a struggling people is acknowledged and respected. Martin Byrne is a Christian Brother working alongside the poor in Dublin's North Inner City and he is convinced that the first task of a Christian community is to get sufficiently close to the poor and begin to recognise some of the many ways in which God is already present in them: "It is often on the margins of society and of the Christian community, such as the life experienced by most in the North Wall, that the presence of the Spirit is most easily understood and discerned" (Byrne, 2008:119).

The Spirit resides in those very places where God's grace is most keenly felt. A closer look at the history of the people of the

North Wall in the North Inner City, Dublin reveals the extent to which their story and the residual impact of the social upheaval that they have had to contend with remain untold. The North Wall was once a thriving community with its proximity to the port and the railway line. With the advent of the containership of port traffic, chronic unemployment and questionable housing policy destabilised the community for a long time. In recent years, the people campaigned for the regeneration of the North Wall and the de-tenanting of the flats and have worked tirelessly to eradicate the scourge of drugs in their community. Byrne sees beyond the veneer of poverty and glimpses the presence of something indefinable that exudes from the humanity of the people of the North Wall: "I have become more convinced that holiness is no longer an elite characteristic of those schooled in spiritual direction, of those engaged in frequent sacramental practice or of those called to clerical or religious lifestyles. Rather it is the stuff of ordinary people challenging each other to be servants and disciples of human community living" (Byrne, 2008:102).

Grace produces a parallel history, not the one that is written, but the one that is experienced in the hidden part of the world. Here, in the shadows, human dignity is salvaged against the odds and is revealed quietly and without embellishment to the world: "There is a mystery in the heart of the poor ... Hidden in their radical poverty, in their obvious wounds, is the mystery of the presence of God" (Vanier, 1979:43). God's grace, once experienced, seeps through to the inner caverns of those receptive to its power and unearths from within the profound human impulse to love. Our solidarity with the poor sets this process in motion: "It may be a meeting with a poor person, whose call awakens a response in us; we discover that there is a living spring hidden deep within us ... the first experience stays hidden in the heart's memory. We know from then on that our deepest life is light and love" (Vanier, 1979:47). Left to our own devices, human beings are fundamentally weak and slip unerringly into accumulating for self to the point of minimising our concern for others: "Of ourselves and by ourselves we cannot leave ourselves and surrender in altruistic love to another; the weight of our free spirit, its existential drive, is to subordinate all else to ourselves" (Haight, 1985:148).

When we create opportunities in life that allow us to bear the burdens of others, we take the first unfaltering steps from egoism to love. It is then we begin to perceive a power greater than we can fully understand at play in our lives: "Loving others is a spiritual force drawing us to union with God ... Whenever we encounter another person in love, we learn something new about God. Whenever our eyes are opened to acknowledge the other, we grow in the light of faith and knowledge of God" (Pope Francis, 2013:133).

Small Christian communities draw on those very reserves needed to release God's grace into the world. Viewed as a whole, these communities appear as a vast kaleidoscope of God's grace, yet, when the lens is narrowed, we see how grace finds its own distinctive pattern in each community. Members of 'The Waterford Omagh Peace Choir' are actively involved in a fundraising campaign to meet the needs of children who were left orphaned in Sri Lanka in the wake of the tsunami in 2004. Three years ago, twenty-four choir members visited Sri Lanka to oversee the building of some of the new orphanages that they were funding and to meet with the children who were already living in the completed homes. The children in Sri Lanka mesmerised them with their smiles, their gestures of kindness and their determination to succeed in life. Lesley Caldwell, one of the team of Directors, reveals the reward that comes from working on these projects and the lasting impression these children have made on her life: "Our time in Sri Lanka was a life changing experience for everyone in the choir. The children are born into situations where the odds are stacked against them from the start. It is they who captivated us with the resilience and warmth of their spirit and we who were truly humbled."

The poor open the pores of our humanity to the gift of grace. On the margins, we come face to face with the truth about ourselves and witness the daily triumph of the human spirit no matter how severe the enveloping storm: "We see the immense reserves of strength and courage in the poor. There is so much to admire in the way people endure and go on, despite adversity, and in the way they remain cheerful, loving, content despite suffering. These are all sacramental moments, signs of Christ's presence in the world" (Waller, 2010:48-49).

The choir was formed in the aftermath of a terrorist attack that claimed thirty-one lives in Omagh in 1998 and is comprised of Catholics and Protestants from Omagh in Northern Ireland and from Waterford in Southern Ireland who believe that what unites them as Christians is far more powerful than anything that could divide them. The collective power of their diverse voices when they sing in Taizé vigils and concerts around Ireland is a potent symbol of their shared aspiration for a new style of society on this island where difference and discord gives way to something more inclusive and harmonious. The choir has been invited to sing in Messines, Belgium at a commemoration to mark the 100th anniversary of 'The 1914 Christmas Peace Truce'. Caldwell reflects on the importance of keeping alive the memory of all that happened that Christmas Eve night: "I cannot imagine what it would have felt like when the silence that hovered over the trenches was interrupted by the sound of a lone tenor voice singing 'Silent Night'. Both sides left the sanctuary of the trenches, walked across 'no man's land' and played football together. Two opposing factions momentarily glimpsed their shared humanity and the absurdity of what they were part of." Music stirs the soul and transports us effortlessly beyond our normal boundaries into the realm of the sacred. The men of 'The 1914 Christmas Peace Truce' remind us that peace can prevail even against the bleakest of backdrops. The hushed murmurings of their song can still be heard. The Christian story and the story of its people collided powerfully yet poignantly that night. Something timeless spilled out onto the battlefields that must never be forgotten.

Now is the moment of truth, the time for decisive action. The Church can only leave the inexcusable failings of its past behind when it discovers in the humanity of its people the source of its redemption. The unique energies of communities at the grassroots provide an opening for God's grace to breathe new life into the Church's mission in the world today: "It is in the lives and action of such groups that the motor and dynamism for the renewal and reformation of the church is to be found. Given the sense of depression that pervades Ireland at this moment, the fact that they can emerge and continue at all is itself a triumph of grace, as well as an invitation to hope, and even to conversion, for the church as a whole" (O'Brien, 1994:136-137). Two decades on and the institutional Church here has yet to fully embrace the possibilities that these communities present.

Humble service rather than a blind adherence to the formulas of old unlocks the pathway to the future. The message the Church proclaims was never meant to have been announced triumphantly to the world. Instead, it reveals its native colours in quiet, unheralded acts of human compassion: "But we have to remind ourselves that we are not saviours. We are simply a tiny sign, among thousands of others, that love is possible ... that there is hope, because we believe that the Father loves us and sends his Spirit to transform our hearts so that we can live everyday life as brothers and sisters" (Vanier, 1979:231).

Archbishop Óscar Romero

The Living Legacy

O n 24 March, 1980, Archbishop Óscar Romero of El Salvador was celebrating Mass in the Chapel of the Hospital de la Divina Providencia. During the Mass, at

6.25pm local time, a lone gunman entered the chapel and killed the Archbishop with a single shot. Monseñor Romero, as he was affectionately known to his people, fell to the ground beneath the large crucifix that was hanging behind the altar. At the end of his radio homily the previous evening, Romero had urged the Salvadoran military to lay down their arms, cease the repression and realise that they were not obliged to carry out orders to kill and maim their own people. His defence of the poor had catapulted him into the eye of the storm. The regime could not tolerate his defiant voice any longer; the flame of insurrection needed to be doused at its source. The killer was a professional hitman carrying out a contract killing for those in power. In an instant, all had changed irrevocably. The pastor of the people had been silenced. Two weeks before his murder, Romero anticipated his impending assassination but offered a message of hope to his people: "If they kill me, I shall rise again in the Salvadoran people. I am not boasting; I say it with the greatest humility ... if God accepts the sacrifice of my life, then may my blood be the seed of liberty, and a sign of the hope that will soon become a reality ... A bishop will die, but the church of God - the people – will never die" (Romero in Sobrino, 1990:100-101).

The tension between grassroots Christian communities and the ruling elite in El Salvador had escalated to crisis proportions in the years before Óscar Romero became archbishop in February 1977. Catholic priests, nuns, teachers and lay workers had been arrested, tortured, beaten and killed for siding with the poor and spurring them onwards to believe that they could one day own their own land and earn a fair wage. Retribution would ruthlessly befall anyone who dared to sow seeds of discontent. The struggle for land dates to the Spanish conquest and the decision taken by governing powers in 1881 to abolish communal land rights in order to allow the coffee magnates to consolidate their holdings. The process of land theft continued until 1932, when the indigenous rose up to challenge the coffee barons' protectors, the Salvadoran military. In what Salvadorans refer to as 'the massacre,' the army responded viciously. More than 30,000 people were killed in one month. In her book *Under the Eagle*, Jenny Peace estimates that by 1961, 12% of the peasants were landless; by 1971, 30% were landless; and by 1980, 65% were landless (Pearce, 1981:209).

Romero came into office a year after a minimal land reform programme was initiated by the army colonel President Arturo Armando Molina, but efforts to redress the imbalance were impeded by the military might of the large plantation owners who responded with extreme force when the need arose. At this time, fourteen families controlled over 60% of the arable land in El Salvador. The ruling oligarchy felt threatened by the unnerving disquiet that was being drummed up on the outer realms of their dominion. Violence and terror were unleashed with uncompromising ferocity to stem the mounting discord. Few were safe.

The *Communidades Ecclesiales de Base* were deemed by the authorities to be too closely associated with the peasant unions and were targeted by the armed forces in an attempt to quell the unrest. The prospect of a once obedient people taking their destiny into their own hands provoked a response. The priests and the people stood shoulder to shoulder in unswerving solidarity undeterred by the threats and the intimidation. The Gospel was their point of reference in an increasingly precarious and uncertain world: "Some priests, seeing in the peasant unions a hope for social justice through political pressure, encouraged their development and themselves spoke of social justice and hope for a better world in their preaching. The Christian communities through their Bible study and discussions made peasants more aware of the misery in which they had to live and the hope, founded on the message of Jesus Christ, of achieving a more decent life" (Brockman, 1984:450). Many priests were prevented from visiting their parishioners and many communities of Christians were unable to meet together for worship and Bible study, especially in the countryside. Church buildings, schools, convents, the Church's radio station and the Catholic university were all in the line of fire. The regime vented its fury through the callous onslaught of machine guns and bombs. The Church at the grassroots in El Salvador was under threat; the impetus for change that was gathering pace would be stifled no matter what the cost.

Archbishop Óscar Romero has been an inspiration to generations of advocates of human rights and social justice all over the world. Hope whispers resoundingly wherever Romero's name is mentioned. His memory is regularly conjured up in the dances, songs, poems and theatre performances of the Salvadoran people, and on the murals and posters that cover the walls of their cities. The poor of El Salvador still feel his presence among them. His courage raised the spirits of an embattled people and continues to galvanise the hopes of the downtrodden around the world today. The words of Michael D. Higgins, President of Ireland, on his recent visit to El Salvador encapsulate the enduring significance of all that Romero lived and died for: "Thus Óscar Romero has become an illuminating icon not only for the Church but for the oppressed of the world and those in solidarity with them" (Higgins, M.D., 2013:17). Monseñor Romero took the circuitous route on the road to his enlightenment. Seminal moments in his life changed the course of his ministry. It is time to re-trace his steps so that we too can begin to steer the Church closer to where it was always meant to be. His legacy lives on in those who walk in his way.

Transformation starts from within – A faith that is open to change

When Óscar Romero was installed as archbishop of San Salvador on February 22, 1977, the consensus was that Romero would drift inauspiciously into the slipstream of the ruling elite and conform to the norms that they imposed. Many viewed his appointment as a victory for the conservative oligarchy and expected him to rein in the subversives who were inciting the poor to become more vehement in their defence of their rights. His allegiance to Rome would inevitably lead him down the path of least resistance. So it appeared! Recalling the dread felt when he was elected and the likelihood that the hierarchy would become even more removed from the struggles of the people in El Salvador, Sobrino observed how "we all thought we faced a very bleak future" (Sobrino, 1990:5).

Romero feared that if the Church re-located to the margins, it risked aggravating the simmering antagonism between the state and the poor. To take sides would ultimately compromise the Church's potential to heal conflict and to dismantle historic barriers between opposing factions. Even when he witnessed for himself the repression and suffering inflicted on the poor in the early years of his tenure as bishop of Santiago de Maria, he was reluctant to speak out publically against the violence preferring to interpret the killings as 'an aberration' that "would be stopped once the government knew what was happening" (Dennis, Golden, Wright, 2000:9). Not surprisingly, his elevation in the Church was greeted at the grassroots with a collective sigh of resignation.

Gradually, though, a new voice rose within Romero as he came face to face with the sinister subworld of violence somewhat obscured beneath the daily grind of the coffee plantations in Santiago de Maria. Many workers who dared to raise their heads above the parapet and voice their legitimate needs and rights simply vanished without trace in a brutal showing of strength by the army. Most were never seen again. The troops were responding to their commands of their superiors whilst those they served cowered shamefully in the shadows of their crimes. Romero soon realised that the disappearances, the torture, the beatings and the murders were all part of an orchestrated campaign by the coffee barons and their allies in government to safeguard their land and their wealth. The seeds of future intolerance of injustice began to germinate internally at first and more overtly in time. Romero struggled to reconcile his concerns as pastor to his people with the stark and violent realities that they had to contend with. He became more forthright in his denunciation of the campaign of terror wreaked upon the peasants and made his home and diocesan buildings a shelter for those in need of refuge: "Slowly, the impoverished and violated people of his diocese led him to a better understanding of the reality they lived. Moved by compassion, he began to feel the fire of righteous anger stir in his soul and to distance himself from the powerful ones who maintained the status quo" (Dennis, Golden, Wright, 2000:9).

The murder of Fr. Rutilio Grande within three weeks of Romero's installation as archbishop proved to be a defining moment in the life and ministry of Óscar Romero. Rutilio worked with a team of seminarians and catechists in Aguilares, a rural parish with a population of 30,000, building a cluster of tightly knit Christian communities to shield the people from their persecution and to guide them forward in their struggle for liberation. Here, thirty-five *haciendas*, or land owners, used most of the flat land in the area for sugar cane and left the rocky hillsides to the *campesinos*, or tenants, who were only paid during the cane harvest. The great majority were economically poor. They lived in very cramped dwellings without electric light, running water, adequate sanitation and toilets. This reflected the national pattern of a country where vast tracts of land were owned by the few who plundered the natural resources of the land and the reserves of the people to secure profitable yields in sugar, coffee or cotton.

Rutilio was a thorn in the side of the authorities. He questioned the machinations of a society that permitted the rich to profit from the captivity of the poor. A cruel irony was unfolding daily in Aguilares as those who reaped the harvest for the rich returned to the wretchedness of the hillsides each evening hungry and dispirited beyond endurance. Rutilio understood that the ideology which perpetuated such misery needed to be confronted head on: "This approach by Rutilio and his team inevitably brought them into conflict with those who were afraid that the peasants would organise, become self-confident and informed, and rise up against their suffering and exploitation" (O'Sullivan, 2002:2).

Rutilio's outspokenness on behalf of the economically poor led to his dismissal by the bishops from his post as lecturer in pastoral theology and director of the social action programme in the seminary. Even the hierarchy had turned its back on him. The people of Aguilares, in contrast, clasped his message of hope to their hearts. They started to believe in possibilities beyond their destitution: "Rutilio, in his sermons, denounced the injustice of a few dominating and exploiting the many for their own profit; and the experience of learning to apply the lessons of the Bible to their own lives was already opening the eyes and lifting the aspirations of the peasants" (Brockman, 1990:9).

Around 5pm on March 12, 1977, Rutilio set out from Aguilares to a rural outpost of his parish in nearby El Paisnal to say the evening Mass. The three-mile journey from Aguilares to El Paisnal took Rutilio along a road of dirt and stone between two fields of sugar cane. Two companions from Aguilares, Manuel, seventy-two years old, and Nelson, a fourteen-year-old who suffered from epilepsy, began the journey with him. Rutilio knew the road well as El Paisnal was the little town where he was born and grew up. His father had been the local mayor a number of times and some of his relatives still lived there. Rutilio's unflinching commitment to the poor and their cause made him a prime target of the rich and the powerful. The agitator needed to be silenced if order was to be restored: "He was vulnerable. He knew that. He had been warned that his life was in danger, and suspicious people had been seen around the parish the very day he was due to say the evening Mass in El Paisnal. He was not deterred. The people would be waiting. He would go to them" (O'Sullivan, 2002:3).

Speaking on the twenty-fifth anniversary of the murder of Rutilio Grande, Michael O'Sullivan, a fellow Jesuit with Rutilio in El Salvador at that time, recalled what happened on the journey to El Paisnal. En route, Rutilio stopped his Volkswagen Safari to give three young children a lift. As he drove off again, it became apparent that a pick-up truck was following them. Ahead they saw a blue car with California plates. The car was stopped and there were men on either side of the road with some form of weapons by their sides. The pick-up accelerated and came up menacingly right behind them. Rutilio and his companions were clearly in danger. One of the men by the side of the road lit a cigarette. This was the signal for murder. The bullets came from both sides as well as from behind. They went into Rutilio's neck and head and into his lower back and pelvis. They also killed old Manuel who appeared to try and shield Rutilio. The children in the back survived. They were allowed to run away. As they did so, a further shot was fired. It killed Nelson who had suffered an epileptic seizure, but was, apparently, still alive: "Today three small crosses mark the spot along the road where Rutilio and his companions were killed. No greater love persons can have than to lay down their life for those they have chosen as their friends. Rutilio Grande died for God and some of the poorest people in the world" (O'Sullivan, 2002:3).

Romero was close friends with Rutilio, and, whilst he empathised with the plight of the campesinos in Aguilares, he nevertheless had deep reservations about Rutilio's pastoral ministry there. His work seemed to be too political and in danger of becoming too closely associated with the revolutionary wing of the peasant movement. Romero feared that Rutilio's style of evangelisation would only stir up an already volatile situation. Rutilio never deviated from his course. His people were his compass. The experience of viewing Rutilio's body and witnessing the despair of the people that evening in Aguilares jolted Romero to the core. The shockwaves that followed would never subside. Romero felt the profound desolation of the poor who had lost their leader in Rutilio. Their shared grief united the pastor with his people like never before. The spirit of Rutilio was etched in the faces of those before him: "There is not a sound as the archbishop walks up the aisle to the spot where the three bodies lie beneath white sheets before the altar. After Romero prays he turns to begin Mass, and he looks out at the faces of the poor. Hundreds of peasants stare back at him. They say nothing. Their silence interrogates Romero. The peasants' eyes ask the question he alone can answer: Will you stand with us as Rutilio did?" (Dennis, Golden, Wright, 2000:29).

Romero had reached the edge of the precipice; in an anonymous chapel on the darkest of evenings his life was stripped of all that once defined him. Rutilio challenged the Monseñor in death as he did in life. In his inner depths, Romero was arriving at his own epiphany. Sobrino observed that as Romero "stood gazing at the mortal remains of Rutilio Grande, the scales fell from his eyes." (Sobrino, 1990:10) The 'scales' were fear of anything that might "immerse the church in the ambiguous, conflictive flesh of history." (Sobrino, 1990:8) For Sobrino, the moment was decisive: "I believe that the murder of Rutilio Grande was the occasion of the conversion of Archbishop Romero ... It was Rutilio's death that gave Archbishop Romero the strength for new activity... and the fundamental direction for his own life" (Sobrino, 1990:9-10). The man who was normally reticent in larger crowds dropped his defences in helpless bewilderment at all that he surveyed. In an act of unscripted spontaneity, Romero drew nearer to those in need of his embrace. He chose not to eulogise about his friendship with Rutilio but rather to place the sacrifice of Rutilio, Manuel and Nelson within God's liberating plan for the people of Aguilares. For Romero, standing as a bystander to the suffering of his people was no longer an option. A peasant pastoral worker could sense the catharsis that was taking place before the intuitive gaze of the people: "As we listened to him we were very surprised. "He has the same voice as Father Grande!" we all said. Because it seemed that at that moment the voice of Father Rutilio passed to Monseñor. Right then and there. Really" (Ernestina Rivera in Dennis, Golden, Wright, 2000:27).

The transformation was not completed that night, but it had begun. Romero consulted with the clergy of the archdiocese and began a series of initiatives that openly defied what the government expected of him. He decided to have one single commemorative Mass for Rutilio, the young boy and the elderly farmer in the plaza outside the cathedral in San Salvador which was attended by over 100,000 people; he made public his support for all priests who were in danger of persecution; he demanded that the government investigate the murders and promised the people that the Church would be on their side; he suspended classes for three days in all Catholic schools and publically promised that he would not participate in official government functions until these crimes had been solved and the repression had been stopped. As archbishop, he never attended an official event from that day onwards. The cry of the people in Aguilares that night was his call to service. The baton had been passed on from one friend to the next. Nothing would obstruct him on his way. God's guiding love was closer than he had realised: "From his new starting point in the poor, Archbishop Romero discovered that God is theirs — their defender, their liberator. Among the poor he discovered that God is God become small — a suffering God, a crucified God. But this also led him to sound the depths of the mystery of an ever greater, transcendent God, the last reserve of truth, goodness, and humanity, on whom we human beings can rely" (Sobrino, 1990:16).

Truths made known in times of crisis

Violence and terror cast a dark shadow over El Salvador. During the first two years of his governance, 30,000 were killed. Romero exposed the insidious harshness of a regime that sought to terrify the people into submission. The Monseñor and his people refused to surrender. In his weekly homilies, he named the massacres and tortures, unmasking the hideousness of a war directed against civilians. The archdiocese's radio station carried his words to most of El Salvador except when bombs silenced it or government jamming interfered with its transmissions. His voice, though somewhat hushed at first, rose in righteous condemnation at the campaign of violence waged against the poor.

Romero opened the doors of the archbishop's residence to the besieged people of his homeland and opted to live in a simple room in the grounds of the nearby hospital. He travelled extensively to meet the people and they, in their multitudes, converged on his offices in San Salvador to meet with him. He listened to their stories of killings, of loved ones taken away, of homes burned and crops destroyed. It was the poor especially who filled his cathedral at Sunday Mass and greeted him afterwards, who came out to meet him when he visited their villages, who encouraged him in hundreds of simple letters. They reminded him of what was essential. Their courage and humanity had transfigured the landscape of all he once knew: "Being incarnate in the real world, Archbishop Romero discovered the deepest of this world's truths: the poverty that cries to heaven. This poverty had concrete faces, and these faces were beloved to him: children dying, campesinos with neither land nor rights, slum-dwellers, the tortured corpses of his people, whose only crime had been their desire to break free of poverty and oppression" (Sobrino, 1990:194).

Closeness to the poor instilled a new confidence in Romero. The ambivalence of the past gave way to a clear resolve to speak his truth boldly and without equivocation. The poor had stirred something deep within. Their pain moved him and disturbed him, both in equal measure: "These poor persons broke his heart, and the wound never closed" (Sobrino, 1990:195). Photojournalist Jim Harney's recollections of the experience of hearing Romero speak capture the imperishable warmth that existed between Romero and the poor: "When Romero entered the cathedral and walked down the aisle, he was followed by applause. It was as if he himself was the word of hope even before he spoke. And then when he spoke ... leading up to the point when he would list the deaths and assassinations of the week, the clapping would swell to a crescendo ... the audience became part of the homily's force and imagination" (Harney in Dennis, Golden, Wright, 2000:36). A beautiful new alliance was forged: "His people filled his heart. He let himself be loved, and this is the most radical way to span distances and burst boundaries, which always exist between those of high and low estate" (Sobrino, 1990:35). God's grace had crept into his world and awakened him from his slumber in ways he least expected. Everything had turned full circle; the poor had become the source of his liberation: "He fairly rushed to the poor, in order to receive from them, to learn from them, and to enable them to impart to him the good news" (Sobrino, 1990:34).

Romero did not lecture the people but articulated their concerns and their fears. At the peak of their repression and persecution, Romero urged the poor to find their own prophetic voice. Their voice and his had become one: "If some day they take the radio station away from us, if they close down our newspaper, if they don't let us speak, if they kill all the priests and the bishop too, and you are left, a people without priests, each one of you must be God's microphone, each one of you must be a messenger, a prophet" (Romero in Brockman, 1998:142). As Sobrino comments, "The impact of words like these on the people was like a jolt of electric current" (Sobrino, 1990:35). In an interview conducted by Marie Adele Dennis with Romero, he alludes to how the poor had wrestled him free from his self-imposed exile: "Their plight began to gnaw at my soul. I began to see with new eyes what was happening. I began to hear in a new way what my priests closest to the poor were saying." (Dennis, 1997:27).

The poor led him to a new vantage point from where he could see more clearly. Their dignity, their sense of humour in spite of their terror, their resilience in the face of unimaginable hardship revealed a deeper mystery. The agony and anguish of the people was Christ's suffering on the cross laid bare in the world: "The face of Christ is among the sacks and baskets of the farmworker; the face of Christ is among those who are tortured and mistreated in prisons; the face of Christ is dying of hunger in the children who have nothing to eat; the face of Christ is in the poor who ask the church for their voice to be heard" (Romero, 1978:327).

Romero invited the poor to critically engage in the historical reality in which they lived so that they would come to grasp the root cause of their oppression and its tragic consequences. He was in no doubt that a more organised, educated people would one day become architects of their own history. Acts of kindness and mercy only reached so far. Romero initiated pastoral programmes that provided the poor with opportunities to improve their skills and understand their entitlements. He was convinced that education of this kind would serve as a necessary precursor to social change. An empowered people could anticipate the steps necessary to scale new horizons. Romero's pastoral letters and homilies called on the people to become participants in their troubled history and to generate a new hope into their shattered communities: "The world of the poor teaches us that liberation will arrive only when the poor are not simply on the receiving end of handouts from governments or from the churches, but when they themselves are the masters and protagonists of their own struggle and liberation" (Romero, 1985:184). Romero stood firm, steadfast in his conviction that their solidarity and love was strong enough to withstand the tumult and the persecution. His words had the power to reassure: "Let us not tire of preaching love; it is the force that will overcome the world. Let us not tire of preaching love. Though we see that waves of violence succeed in drowning the fire of Christian love, love must win out; it is the only thing that can" (Romero in Brockman, 1998:7).

Access to truths of timeless importance often comes through the darker corridors of suffering and despair. Romero penetrated through the layers of confusion and turmoil and arrived at a new clarity. His wisdom was translated into a language that people could understand. His antennae leaned towards the poor as he reached out to them in a spirit of love and respect. The people no longer languished on the sidelines: "Let us not measure the church by the number of its members or by its material buildings ... The material walls here will be left behind in history. What matters is you, the people, your hearts" (Romero in Brockman, 1998:24). What was happening in the *Communidades Ecclesiales de Base* across El Salvador was a microcosm of what was needed in the Church the world over. The unique energies at the grassroots inspired Romero to glimpse all that could be achieved when those once silenced seize the initiative and allow their creative vision flow through the life of the Church. He could see that the catalyst for the reform in the Church must come from the people if it was going to have real impact: "Don't be waiting for which way the bishop will lean, or for what others will say, or what the organization says ... You have to be critical and see the world and individuals using your own judgment and Christians must learn to sharpen their distinctive Christian judgment" (Romero in Brockman, 1998:178).

A Church that bears the force of Love

Romero's return to Aguilares three months after the murder of Rutilio would put him on a collision course with the ruling authorities. The people needed a sign that an end of their tyranny was in sight. Hope was fast dissolving into the ether of a bloodshot sky. Their spiritual home was under siege. The army had occupied the parish, killing the sacristan, expelling a foreign priest and turning the church into a military barracks. How would Romero respond? Any action on his part to repel the hostility and reclaim the church would have consequences and he knew it. Oblivious to the on-looking troops, he entered the church, walked purposefully towards the now desecrated altar and addressed the multitudes that followed him: "You are the image ... of Christ, nailed to the cross and lanced by the spear. You are a symbol of every town, like Aguilares, that will be struck down and trampled upon; but if you suffer with faith and give your suffering a redemptive meaning, Aguilares will be singing the precious song of liberation" (Romero in Dennis, Golden, Wright, 2000:41).

The Eucharist was shared out among the people. During Mass, he imparted the Word. After Mass, he exemplified its significance. A procession was held from the church out into the open square where the military had gathered. Romero held the Blessed Sacrament aloft and the people led the way. Sobrino was present in Aguilares that day and captures the magnitude of the moment: "As the procession drew near the town hall we stopped. We were uneasy. In fact, we were afraid. We had no idea what might happen. And we all instinctively turned around and looked at Archbishop Romero, who was bringing up the rear, holding the monstrance. 'Adelante (Forward!),' said Archbishop Romero. And we went right ahead. The procession ended without incident. From that moment forward, Archbishop Romero was the symbolic leader of El Salvador" (Sobrino, 1990:27-28).

The people and their pastor, in that instant, had disarmed the troops and rendered their aggression futile. Their victory, though fleeting, would keep the flame of hope alive. Romero believed that the Gospel, by its very nature, needed to be vindicated in the midst of the historical struggle of his people. He understood that the Word finds its deepest resonance when absorbed into the turbulent realities of each new age: "Some want to keep a Gospel so disembodied that it doesn't get involved at all in the world it must save. Christ is now in history. Christ is in the womb of the people. Christ is now bringing about the new heavens and the new earth" (Romero in Brockman, 1998:102). Implicit in Romero's theology is a belief that civilisation is incomplete and that God's work is unfinished. God wishes to bring the story of civilisation to a point where humanity no longer has to endure persecution and suffering and the El Salvadoran people are integral to this task: "God and human beings make history. God saves humanity in the history of one's own people. The history of salvation will be El Salvador's history when we Salvadorans seek in our history the presence of God the Savior" (Romero in Brockman, 1998:173). Romero's embodiment of the Word became the most potent feature of his ministry. His witness paved the way for others to follow: "Archbishop Romero was a gospel. Archbishop Romero was a piece of good news from God to the poor of this world, and then from this starting point in the poor, to all men and women" (Sobrino, 1990:58).

Romero could see in the collective synergy of the *Communidades Ecclesiales de Base*, the prayer groups and the peasant unions evidence of a greater power at play in the lives the poor of El Salvador. The activities of the peasant unions, though not explicitly religious in their motivation, were shaping the history of the El Salvadoran people in a way that reflected everything that God intended for them. God's love infiltrates this world in a myriad of ways: "Everyone who struggles for justice, everyone who makes just claims in unjust surroundings is working for God's reign, even though not a Christian. The church does not comprise all of God's reign; God's reign goes beyond the church's boundaries" (Romero in Brockman, 1984:38). Romero repeatedly emphasised the importance of promoting unity and solidarity among the many peasant unions and the base communities so that together they could realise their shared aspirations. The old divides had to yield to something more inclusive and more real: "What we developed as we walked with poor people – campesinos, the homeless, the urban poor – was a new awareness of injustice and a passionate commitment to social transformation. What we encountered was real life – raw, painful, beautiful, sometimes ugly – but real" (Romero in Dennis, 1997:38-39).

A persecuted Church is the supreme sign of the incarnation of Christ's compassion and love for humanity. Nuns, priests, co-ordinators, catechists and pastoral agents in El Salvador at this time shared the same fate as the poor. Romero recognised the powerful symbolism of their sacrifice: "It would be sad that in a country in which there are so many horrible assassinations there were no priests counted among the victims. They are the testimony of a church incarnated in the problems of its people." (Romero in Brockman, 1990:177) With these words he was going against centuries of ecclesiastical tradition that distanced the leaders from their people. He could not tolerate a system that would buy his silence. Rutilio's death had revealed a noble, if unforgiving, truth: "Rutilio taught Óscar, by his death, that he himself must not be different to the people, that he must live his empathy and solidarity with them to the point even of being vulnerable to assassination like them" (O'Sullivan, 2010:2). During his funeral two days after Romero's murder, a bomb went off outside the Cathedral and the panic-stricken mourners were machine-gunned, leaving an estimated thirty to forty people dead and several hundred wounded. The elite were determined to trample on his memory. The bishops of El Salvador stayed at a safe distance. Their absence confirmed their cowardly indifference: "The majority of the bishops had opposed Romero while he was alive, and even though he had been shot dead while celebrating Mass, thus evoking the Last Supper and the bloody death of Jesus on Calvary, these bishops still did not show solidarity with him or the people by taking part in his funeral" (O' Sullivan, 2010:5).

The poor claimed Romero as their own amidst the gunfire and the shells. His crucifixion was theirs to bear. Romero's persecution, like his people's, would herald a new dawn for El Salvador. His untiring quest for a better world remained resolute to the end: "If we follow in his footsteps we shall further the cause of justice and peace, truth and love; we shall help denounce atrocities, destruction, and repression; we shall help to shorten and humanize our wars; we shall defend the cause of the poor throughout the world - and certainly, in El Salvador, we shall defend the cause of a people that Archbishop Romero loved so much that he gave his life for them" (Sobrino, 1990:201). Romero had the courage to take the road less travelled. The pastor's journey parallels the direction the Church must take if it is to reclaim its credibility in the world. The tribute of fourteen-year-old student, Elena, to Monseñor Romero thirty-four years after his murder says all that needs to be said about the legacy he leaves in his wake. The Monseñor's sacrifice and that of countless others must not be in vain. His spirit lives on in those who sing to the tune of his love.

Poem to
Monseñor Romero

When the shepherd cries out, everything trembles.
When he speaks the truth, all are quiet.
When he begs for justice, they do not bring it ...
Yet, how great is the harvest of love that he sows.

We had in El Salvador a living saint,
Whom they did not want to canonize ...
How can the church silence the voice of the prophet
And not hear his song?

This was Óscar and his love,
Upright man of profound prayer.
I wish today to sound my own song,
And tell him: you live on in this pain.

Gave of himself in living
A saintly and holy life.
Gave of himself with madness,
A madness of loving until death.

Yet, you live on in your people,
You came back to life in your homeland good shepherd.
My generation calls you simply: Monseñor,
May you light up our hearts from the heavens.

(Excerpts from a poem written by fourteen-year-old
student Elena, from the Externado de San José, San
Salvador in Hopper, 2014:7)

Charting a New Course
Steps to the Future

The time for change has arrived. The Church's movement through history has reached a decisive crossroads. To cling rigidly to the ways of old will lead the Church down a road of irreversible decline. The people at the grassroots blaze a new trail and remind us that all is not lost. Slowly, resolutely, a new future is being revealed in the unshakable spirit of those who will no longer stand still and wait for change to happen. Here, in the shadows, everything is distilled right down to the core essentials. The clouds are parting and the light is beginning to shine in ways we never noticed before: "But it is also true that in the midst of darkness something new always springs to life and sooner or later produces fruit. On razed land life breaks through, stubbornly yet invincibly. However dark things are, goodness always re-emerges and spreads" (Pope Francis, 2013:135).

Through the obscurity of the darkened skies, the radiance of the stars becomes more keenly perceptible. The gloom and despondency are yielding to a new hope. Somewhere beneath the shade, a life force beyond what the eye can see is at play. All that once escaped us becomes clear: "It may be winter when the luxurious foliage no longer clothes the trees of piety. But the bare branches enable us to see deeper into the woods. There we see the gracious mystery of God" (Johnson, 2007:46).

Now is the hour to imagine something altogether different from what has existed previously and to take the first tentative steps towards making this a reality. This *kairos* time compels us to cast the net beyond the traditional boundaries of Church and tap into the eclectic energies of groups on the sidelines of the old ecclesial order that are already changing the landscape of their own local communities. The Church needs to discover within the creative reserves of its own people the direction it seeks in this hour of uncertainty and begin to "lend a sharper ear, a keener eye, a livelier anticipation to the slightest indication that somewhere that Spirit is stirring whose inspiration is not merely confined to the official pronouncements and directives of the church" (Rahner, 1992:247). If we dare to reach outside the insular walls of the past, we will begin to discover that what we are searching for is taking shape before our eyes. On the periphery, we glimpse a world of opportunity. Almost unknowingly, the people are showing us the way: "I believe that this is a good time for the church in the Western world to change its overall priority – to change from an attitude of maintenance and servicing of our present practising communities, to what I would call 'frontier work' ... work on and beyond the regular boundaries of the church. This calls for a 'reaching out attitude' and an eagerness to enter what seem like foreign 'worlds', especially the world of the 'unchurched' and the world of those who are engaged in a spiritual search" (Dorr, 2004:205).

The destiny of a small Christian community is not pre-determined from the start but advances naturally over time in symmetry with the qualities and the personality that each individual brings to their community. It is important to facilitate a process of dialogue and consultation from the outset so that the people and not the structures define the way forward: "The organisation is for people, not people for the organisation ... if the structures employed by a group do not help the participants in their efforts to relate to one another, they must be looked at seriously and, when necessary, changed. Persons must come first" (O'Halloran, 2010:74). The community must be given space to breathe so that the spontaneity and unique charisma of each new grouping are not suffocated from the beginning. The danger is that if these communities are pushed too hard in the initial stages, the motivation and drive that propels them onwards will wane in time. Meetings should encourage relaxed interaction and the choice of venue should reflect this informality. The unspoken solidarity between members is the life blood that sustains each community at each phase of its evolution. This is not sealed in an instant. It takes time. What starts out slowly and patiently is more likely to endure.

While small Christian communities can grow organically out of what is happening in the wider social community, sometimes a creative spark is needed to activate the process. The reality is that many Christians feel betrayed by the Church and are reluctant to be tainted by association with the peculiarities of an institution that has lost their trust. The accumulated resentment of the past has left an indelible stain on the present. Something unforced is needed to lead people to a point where they can experience Church as it was always intended to be. The task of evangelising is not about imposing something from the outside but creating the space for people to discover for themselves from within.

The series of initiatives undertaken by an action group in 'The Edmund Rice Heritage Centre', Waterford, illustrate one such way of reaching out to people who have become disheartened with the institutional Church and are open to finding new ways of keeping their faith alive. The group organised a 'Carols for Our Times' and set about promoting the event beyond the normal parameters of Church. Creative posters were designed and distributed around the city, a press release was circulated to local media and members of the action group spread the word through their own local parish communities. Word of mouth proved the most effective marketing tool. On the night, a series of reflections and poems were interspersed with carols led by 'The Waterford Peace Choir' to create a calm yet uplifting spiritual experience. Over 400 people attended the forty-five minute service in the peaceful and candlelit environs of 'The Edmund Rice Chapel'. At the end of the service, one of the team addressed the gathering briefly to encourage anyone interested in attending a workshop on small Christian community early in the new year to leave their contact details as they left. The process of initiating something new had begun.

The goal of the workshop was two-fold; to explore the defining features of a small Christian community and to generate interest in the possibility of forming a new community in the city. The seating was arranged in a circle to facilitate dialogue. In the opening phase of the workshop, one of the facilitators encouraged everyone who attended to introduce themselves and to share their own experience of Church in an informal exchange of views that set the tone for the discussions that were to follow. The second facilitator then made a short presentation, combining a series of photographs with a short commentary, to capture the distinctive dynamics of a small Christian community. Participants were then invited to articulate their own vision of Church in an open forum chaired by one of the facilitators while the second facilitator recorded the insights and observations aired from the floor and gave a synopsis of the recurring ideas at the end of this session. Questions were asked, experiences were recalled and stories were told as the participants processed the information presented to them: "The animating team can share guidelines regarding the practical workings of the communities and the vision that accompanies them ... there is no neat package to unwrap; no clear blueprint ... only ideas and down-to-earth suggestions that can help groups move in the right general direction ... everything said has to be examined by the participants in the light of their own experience, because they have to make it flesh and blood in their situation" (O'Halloran, 2010:76).

During the middle phase of the workshop, Gemma, Yvonne

and Mary from Fatima Mansions, Dublin were invited to share their experience of small Christian community and to shed light on the enduring appeal of the 'The Fig Tree Group' for each of them over the past thirty years. They then led a thirty minute reflective session that eased the participants into experiencing first-hand how the Gospel animates the life of a small Christian community. A candle was lit, a copy of a Gospel passage was handed out to each participant in the workshop, five people were nominated to read a segment each and everyone was given the opportunity to identify a line from the Gospel passage that resonated with them. After a short period of silent reflection, participants were encouraged to articulate how the lines of scripture spoke to them at that time. People felt free to speak and equally under no pressure to do so.

In the final phase, the participants were divided into smaller working groups and were given time to reflect on what they would like to see emerge out of their discussions together. Each group had its own secretary who reported back to the larger assembly in the open feedback session that followed. The workshop had arrived at a point where the participants themselves decided on practical strategies that they deemed necessary to set the process of forming a small Christian community in motion: "Vague intentions are of no use at this point. What is called for are about *four or five precise concrete steps* that will help to launch the groups. So the participants are urged to discern these through dialogue and the guidance of the Holy Spirit" (O'Halloran, 2010:76).

Two weeks later, ten people turned up for the first meeting and a new small Christian community began to find its own distinct footing in the world. They quickly reached consensus on a charter for action that would guide them through the early stages of their development as a community: they agreed to meet once a month on the last Tuesday of each month; leadership would be rotated from one meeting to the next and that person would select a piece of scripture, a poem or song in advance to inspire the reflection and sharing of the group; they would be guided by Pierre Simson's *The Buttonhole Gospels* in their efforts to bring the world of scripture alive; the meeting would last no more than one hour and would finish with a relaxed chat over a cup of tea. From the beginning, outreach to the wider community became a natural extension of their reflective time together. 'The Edmund Rice Small Christian Community' have organised meditative prayer evenings for people undergoing treatment for cancer, they hold Taizé vigils to create a sacred space for people in the locality to come to each month and they campaign for the rights of asylum seekers and other minority groups in Waterford whose voice often goes ignored. One of the founding members of the community reflects on her reasons for making the initial leap of faith: "I'm not sure why I came initially. I just feel a strong need for something more than what I experience in my existing faith world. The team from Fatima Mansions showed me what it is like to belong to a faith community. This sense of belonging is what I have been missing. They struck a deep chord in me that helped me to see that there was another way."

The origins of small Christian communities testify to the value of creating the conditions for people to come together in a reflective, prayerful environment to discuss their views on the style of Christian community that they would like to be part of. Providing the right catalyst gives real impetus to the task of promoting new communities within and beyond the existing arena of Church. If what happens is to flow naturally, it needs to be planned with precision. The guidelines that follow can be adapted to the vagaries and characteristics unique to each group and setting:

- Create an atmosphere that draws people into the realm of the spiritual. Candlelight, elements from the natural world and music all enhance the aesthetic backdrop and can transform any setting into a sacred space.

- The dialogue between the facilitators and the participants is key to ensuring that what happens during the workshop and what grows from it reflect the collective wisdom of all who attend.

- Do not burden participants in the workshop with too much information. Limit the presentation on small Christian community to a short time and consider using photographs and stories to illustrate the points being made.

- It is most beneficial to have people who are members of existing small Christian communities present, or people with direct experience of this style of community, as their testimonies are a powerful means of generating interest in this new model of Church.

- The workshop cannot be hijacked by people with their own negative agenda. Give everyone the chance to speak, to articulate their views on where things have gone wrong, but always manoeuvre discussions towards positive action. The flame of hope must be kept alive.

- It is important to 'anchor' discussions on Church in the context of the pressing challenges of today and to heighten an awareness of the responsibility of Christians to help those who are marginalised and impoverished in the world.

> A creative use of slides or film can help to capture the need to reach out and help those who have no voice in the world.

- Give participants the opportunity to reflect in small groups on a Gospel passage so that they can experience the potential of scripture to open up important truths in life.

- Draw up a specific charter of action at the end of the event and allow the participants to shape and influence the direction their small Christian community takes.

- Above all, make the event as relaxed and informal as possible. The welcome beforehand and the refreshments afterwards put people at their ease from the start and help to establish the camaraderie and friendships that are essential to the life of a small Christian community.

Small Christian communities, once formed, can drift unsuspectingly into their own set routine and easily lose their initial zeal and enthusiasm. Whilst clearly defined programmes are necessary to give shape and direction to meetings, these communities must always be prepared to stretch out beyond their habitual ways when the need arises. If they settle into their own comfort zone, they risk becoming rudderless and bereft of the impetus necessary to move forward with confidence. Each community "emerges, is born, and is continually reshaped" without deviating from the core principles that are fundamental to the life of the community (Boff, 1985:127). A small Christian community is constantly on its journey rather than having reached its destination. It is propelled forward by the creative flair of its people. The goals of each community are the prerogative of the entire community. Everyone has their say: "At this stage the ideal is that different members of the group throw their ideas and suggestions into the common pool, and then 'let them go'. This means that everybody can evaluate and build on the various pooled ideas, scarcely adverting to who first proposed them" (Dorr, 2004:49).

Communities at the grassroots can find themselves increasingly fragmented and isolated in the world and somewhat alienated from the wider network of communities that they belong to. When problems arise, as they inevitably will, it can prove difficult to resolve them without rupturing the bonds of trust and friendship and damaging the unity of the group. Times of trial test the character of the community. Sometimes strong leadership is needed at these moments to hold things together until the storm passes and to ensure that no one person is isolated within the community. The wellbeing of the less vocal members of the community is a good barometer of the cohesion of the group. Often the quieter, more reserved members of the community articulate truths that might otherwise remain unspoken. Their voice must never be stifled: "This 'unlikely' person puts forward the real challenge, or offers a word of wisdom which touches people in their hearts more that at a 'head' level ... Sometimes the other members of the group have great difficulty in 'hearing' such a voice, precisely because they would never expect this rather marginal person to be a channel for prophetic truth" (Dorr, 1996:47-48).

Small Christian communities provide a spiritual homeland for people amidst the confusions and uncertainties of life, a safe place free from hostility and censure. The search for meaning often leads people beyond the secluded sanctuaries of old into the wider amphitheatre of everyday where the infinite source of all life penetrates the finite realities of this world in a special way. Members of these communities come to discover God's love in a myriad of ways: in nature; in historical events; in art, music and dance; in interior peacefulness and exterior healing; in the whole range of human experience, particularly love and loss. Increasingly, people are being drawn into the vast expanse of the unknown in their quest to find the living God: "There is such a hunger for a mature faith in many people today. Women and men yearn for a relationship with the living God commensurate with their aspirations, competencies, and struggles in our perilous times. Stale, naive, worn-out concepts of God no longer satisfy" (Johnson, 2007:2).

These communities make it possible for people to find their own distinct cadence on their faith journey. People may be at different stages on the one pathway, yet no one is more advanced than the other. There is an implicit understanding in the small Christian community that the road to enlightenment can take many twists and turns for everyone and that fate can deal a cruel hand when least expected. Each person finds their own inner compass to steer them on their way: "A contemplative attitude is necessary: it is the feeling that you are moving along the good path of understanding ... profound peace, spiritual consolation, love of God and love of all things in God – this is the sign that you are on this right path" (Pope Francis, 2013:10).

A small Christian community find its strength from within but projects outwards so that the response of its people to the Word becomes a stimulus for transformative action. Christians may reach for the skies but their feet must always remain grounded on all that this world reveals. A love that bears the burdens of the weak and the persecuted seals the mystical union between humanity and God: "It is not enough to say that love of

God is inseparable from the love of one's neighbour. It must be added that love for God is unavoidably expressed through love of one's neighbour" (Gutiérrez, 1988:190). Our Christian faith does not extricate us from the reality of suffering and injustice but strengthens our resolve to take decisive action to change what is no longer tolerable in our world. The radical solidarity with the poor that Jesus asks of us demands nothing less. Dietrich Bonhoeffer illustrates this powerfully: if a horse and carriage break loose and are careering down a busy road leaving a path of destruction behind, what should one do? (Bonhoeffer in Johnson, 2007:83-84). Bending over the injured to bind up their wounds is one necessary and noble deed. But to prevent continuing harm, someone has to grab the reins or jam the wheel spokes and stop the horse. The former is the work of charity; the latter, the praxis of justice. The goal is transformation of social structures, which, while it will never usher in the reign of God completely, will signal its arrival in the boundless reserves of those who work tirelessly for a better world.

The winds of ecclesiastical change are beginning to blow more favourably. The haze is slowly lifting and a new clarity is descending on a once shrouded terrain. All that has defined us to this point cannot dictate the shape of what is to come. An openness to change draws us closer to the source of our renewal: "A tradition that cannot change cannot be preserved. Where people experience God as still having something to say, the lights stay on" (Johnson, 2007:23). If the future of the Church is community, fresh thinking is needed in all sectors of the Church. What is required is a new environment that encourages discussion, debate and even divergence of opinion. To engage in dialogue necessitates a willingness to listen to the dissenting voice and to interact directly with those who may have opposing views on the best way forward for the universal Church at this time. Listening paves the way for new understanding and consolidates common ground. There are signs that this process is slowly starting to happen. Bill Murphy, Bishop of Kerry, calls for those once silenced in the Church to make their voice heard and signals his own commitment to the "empowerment of lay people based on real collaboration at all levels and the inclusion of women in the decision-making in our diocese" (Murphy in O'Hanlon, 2011:100).

The institution and the people cannot be cut off from one another in separate stratospheres. They co-exist and belong together. Rome must learn to permit and encourage a reasonable degree of autonomy in these communities so that each community can exist independently yet feels part of the wider movement of the universal Church. Resources and stories could be shared, new avenues in Christian witness could be promoted and regional assemblies could be organised to foster real co-operation between communities. In short, more could be done to support communities from the time of their inception and to give added impetus and legitimacy to their efforts to draw the Church closer to its source and to its people. The stated objective of the Irish Episcopal Conference (2010) to open up a dialogue "with those who are committed, with those who are interested, with those who are alienated" is a necessary first step in the hierarchy reaching out to the margins (Irish Bishops, 2010:14). Yet this process is merely cosmetic unless all the people, women and men, have their say in determining a new direction for the Church today. Discernment must lead to action. It is futile giving a voice to the people if their perceptions and aspirations are not acted on: "It is a totally new experience for parishioners to be asked for suggested actions, even to mandate a parish meeting. Once the process starts, however, I suspect that most feel that change has begun" (Redmond, 2011:74).

It takes courage to take the decisive steps towards freedom. What is required is a significant gesture to 'kick start' a radical overhaul of the existing dynamic of governance in the Church. The Church needs to be returned to its people. This hour of crisis can herald a new orientation in those very structures that have led us to this point. This is a shift, not a loss. American theologian Paul Lakeland anticipates a day when the traditional parish will be steered by "a small team of ministers, all of whom will have been ordained by the bishop to celebrate the Eucharist" who recognise their "accountability not only to the local bishop ... but most especially to the local community that they serve" (Lakeland, 2003:267-268). German theologian Fritz Lobinger argues that a new style of ordination needs to be introduced for lay co-ordinators, women and men, so that ministers are not a separate class but arise from the ranks of those with a proven record of service to their parish community. The Church then begins to break free from the shackles of its past and liberate its people to shape the path of its future: "All of them wanted to assist the community; they did not aim at priesthood. They do not have a clericalistic outlook; they have proved over many years that their style of leadership is a non-dominating one seeking the cooperation of the whole community" (Lobinger, 1998:69).

Small Christian communities cannot remain entrenched in their own religious ideologies and dismissive of the richness of other faith traditions. The old divisions of the past must yield to something more unifying. In a world exposed to the volatility of religious extremism, faith communities of all persuasions have a role to play in ushering in a new era of reconciliation. Embracing difference opens the mind to universal truths and paves the way for real empathy: "Solidarity, in its deepest and most challenging sense, thus becomes a way of making history in a life setting where conflicts, tensions and oppositions can achieve a life-giving unity" (Pope Francis, 2013:112). After the tsunami of 2004, the town of Matara in Sri Lanka united like never before to bury their dead and to lend practical assistance to each other when the waters receded. Hindu, Muslim and Christian carried each others burdens in mutual solidarity. When diverse faith traditions come together as one to respond to a common plight, it gives rise to a deep cordiality and an appreciation of the one indivisible life force shared by all. It is then we realise that the story of each faith community is part of the great narrative of God's call and humanity's response: "Those who are confident in their faith are not threatened but enlarged by the different ways of others. As we discover deeper truth than what we thought we possessed as a monopoly, the dignity of difference becomes a source of blessing" (Johnson, 2007:179).

Bibliography

Aquino, M. (2002), 'Latina Feminist Theology: Central Features', in Aquino, M., Machado, D. & Rodriguez, J. (eds.), *A Reader in Latina Feminist Theology: Religion and Justice* (Austin: University of Texas Press).

Association of Catholic Priests, (2010), *Objectives* [online], available: http://www.associationofcatholicpriests.ie/objectives/ [September 2010].

Barreiro, A. (1982), *Basic Ecclesial Communities* (New York: Orbis Publications).

Boff, L. (1985), *Church Charism and Power: Liberation Theology and the Institutional Church* (London: SCM Press).

Boff, L. (1986), *Ecclesiogenesis and Church, Charism and Power* (New York: Orbis).

Boff, L. (1989), *Faith on the Edge* (San Francisco: Harper and Row).

Boff, L. (1997), *Ecclesiogenesis – The Base Communities Reinvent the Church* (New York: Orbis Books).

Boff, L. (2007), *Essential Care – An Ethics Of Human Nature*, trans. Guilherme, A. (London: SPCK Publications).

Bohan, H. and Shouldice, F. (2002), *Community and the Soul of Ireland: the Need for Values-Based Change* (Dublin: The Liffey Press).

Brockman, J. (1984), 'Oscar Romero: Shepherd of the Poor', *Third World Quarterly* 6 (2), 446–457.

Brockman, J. (1984), *The Church Is All Of You – Thoughts of Archbishop Oscar Romero* (Minnesota: Winston Press).

Brockman, J. (1990), *Romero: A Life* (New York: Orbis Books).

Brockman, J. (1998), *Oscar Romero: The Violence of Love* (Farmington: The Plough Publishing House).

Brueggemann, W. (1982), *The Prophetic Imagination*, (Philadelphia: Fortress Press).

Byrne, M. (2008), *Freshly Baked Bread – Urban Contextual Communal Theology in Dublin's North Wall 1998–2008* (Dublin: CRM Design and Print).

Comblin, J. (1993), 'The Holy Spirit', trans. Barr, R. in Ellacuría, I. & Sobrino, J. (eds.), *Systematic Theology: Perspectives from Liberation Theology* (New York: Orbis Publications), 146–164.

Comblin, J. (1993), 'Grace', trans. Barr, R. in Ellacuría, I. & Sobrino, J. (eds.), *Systematic Theology: Perspectives from Liberation Theology* (New York: Orbis Publications), 205–215.

Congar, Y. (1988), 'The Church', in Lauret, B. (ed.), *Fifty Years of Catholic Theology: Conversations with Yves Congar* (London: SCM Press), 40–85.

Cooke, B. (1976), *Ministry to Word and Sacrament: History and Theology* (Philadelphia: Fortress Press).

Dennis, M. (1997), *A Retreat With Oscar Romero and Dorothy Day – Walking With the Poor* (Ohio: St. Anthony Messenger Press).

Dennis, M., Golden, R. and Wright, S. (2000), *Oscar Romero – Reflections on His Life and Writings* (New York: Orbis Books).

Dorr, D. (1996), *Divine Energy – God Beyond Us, Within Us, Among Us* (Dublin: Gill and Macmillan).

Dorr, D. (2004), *Time for a Change – A fresh look at Spirituality, Sexuality, Globalisation and the Church* (Dublin: Columba Press).

Dorr, D. (2006), *Spirituality of Leadership – Inspiration, Empowerment, Intuition and Discernment* (Dublin: Columba Press).

Dulles, A. (1983), *A Church to Believe In: Discipleship and the Dynamics of Freedom* (New York: The Crossroad Publishing Company).

Ellis, M. and Maduro, O. (1989), *The Future of Liberation Theology: Essays in Honour of Gustavo Gutiérrez* (New York: Orbis Books).

Ferro, C. (1981) 'The Latin American Woman: The Praxis and Theology of Liberation, in Torres, S. & Eagleson, J. (eds.), *The Challenge of Basis Christian Communities* (New York: Orbis Publications), 24–37.

Freire, P. (1970), *Pedagogy of the Oppressed* (New York: The Continuum Publishing Company).

Fuellenbach, J. (1995), *The Kingdom Of God: The Message of Jesus Today* (New York: Orbis Books).

Ganiel, G. (2012), 'Loss and Hope in the Irish Catholic Church: Part 11', *Doctrine and Life*, 62 (5), 35–46.

Groome, T. (1980), *Christian Religious Education – sharing our story and vision*, (San Francisco: Harper and Row Publishers).

Gutiérrez, G. (1973), *A Theology of Liberation* (New York: Orbis Books).

Gutiérrez, G. (1981), 'The Irruption of the Poor in Latin America and the Christian Communities of the Common People', in Torres, S. & Eagleson, J. (eds.), *The Challenge of Basis Christian Communities* (New York: Orbis Publications), 107–123.

Gutiérrez, G. (1983), *The Power of the Poor in History* (New York: Orbis Books).

Gutiérrez, G. (1986/1990), *The Truth Shall Make You Free*, (New York: Orbis Books).

Gutiérrez, G. (1988), *A Theology of Liberation* (London: SCM Press).

Gutiérrez, G. (1991), *The God of Life* (New York: Orbis Books).

Gutiérrez, G. (1993), 'Option for the Poor', trans. Barr, R. in Ellacuría, I. & Sobrino, J. (eds.), *Systematic Theology: Perspectives from Liberation Theology* (New York: Orbis Publications), 22–37.

Gutiérrez, G. (2005), *We Drink from our Own Wells* (London: SCM Press).

Haight, R. (1985), *An Alternative Vision: An Interpretation Of Liberation Theology* (New York: Paulist Press).

Haight, R. (2001), *Dynamics of Theology* (New York: Orbis Books).

Higgins, M. D., (2013), *Of Memory And Testimony – The Importance of Paying Tribute to Those Who Were Emancipatory* (San Salvador: La Universidad Centroamericana).

Hopper, J. (2014), 'Risk, prophecy, truth and inspiration: a picture of

Archbishop Romero in the education system of El Salvador', in *International Studies in Catholic Education*, 6 (1): 4–13.

Irish Bishops (2010), *Share the Good News: National Directory for Catechesis in Ireland* (Dublin: Veritas).

Johnson, E. A. (2007), *Quest For The Living God – Mapping Frontiers In The Theology Of God* (London: Bloomsbury Publishing).

Kirby, P. (1981), *Lessons in liberation* (Dublin: Dominican Publications).

Küng, H. (2013), *Can We Save The Church? – We Can Save The Church!* (London: William Collins).

Lakeland, P. (2003), *The Liberation of the Laity. In Search of an Accountable Church* (New York: Continuum Publishing Company).

Lernoux, P. (1979), 'The Long Path to Puebla', in Eagleson, J. & Scharper, P. (eds.), *Puebla and Beyond* (New York: Orbis Publications), 3–27.

Lobinger, F. (1998), *Like His Brothers and Sisters – Ordaining Community Leaders* (New York: The Crossroads Publishing Company).

Magaña, A. Q. (1993), 'Ecclesiology in the Theology of Liberation', trans. Barr, R. in Ellacuría, I. & Sobrino, J. (eds.), *Systematic Theology: Perspectives on Liberation Theology* (New York: Orbis Publications), 178–193.

Mannion, G. (2007), 'New Wine and New Wineskins: Laity and a Liberative Future for the Church', *International Journal of Practical Theology*, 11 (2), 193–211.

McAfee Brown, R. (1990), *Gustavo Gutiérrez: An Introduction to Liberation Theology* (New York: Orbis Books).

McGovern, A. (1989), *Liberation Theology and Its Critics: Towards an Assessment* (New York: Orbis Publications).

McVerry, P. (2003), *The Meaning is in the Shadows*, (Dublin: Veritas).

McVerry, P. (2003), Mary's Vision of Justice' in Jesuit Centre for Faith and Justice, *Windows on Social Spirituality* (Dublin: Columba Press).

McVerry, P. (2006), 'Responding to Spiritual Hunger?', in Bohan, H. (ed.), *Filling the Vacuum?* (Dublin: Veritas), 67–76.

McVerry, P. (2008), *Jesus: Social Revolutionary?* (Dublin: Veritas).

Medellin: Second General Conference of Latin American Bishops (1968), *The Church in the Present-Day. Transformation of Latin America in the Light of the Council, 11: Conclusions* (Washington D.C.: USCC)

Mesters, C. (1981), 'The Use of the Bible in Christian Communities of the Common People', in Torres, S. & Eagleson, J. (eds.), *The Challenge of Basis Christian Communities*, 197–212, (New York: Orbis Publications).

Moltmann, J. (1979), *The Future of Creation: Collected Essays*, trans. Kohl, M., (Philadelphia: Fortress Press).

Muñoz, R. (1981), 'Ecclesiology in Latin America', in Torres, S. & Eagleson, J. (eds.), *The Challenge of Basic Christian Communities* (New York: Orbis Publications), 150–160.

Nickoloff, J. (1993), 'Church of the Poor: The Ecclesiology of Gustavo Gutiérrez', *Theological Studies*, 54, 512–535.

Nickoloff, J. (1996), *Gustavo Gutiérrez: Essential Writing* (New York: Orbis Books).

O'Brien, J. (1994), *Seeds of a New Church* (Dublin: Columba Press).

O'Halloran, J. (2010), *Living Cells: Vision and Practicalities of Small Christian Communities and Groups* (Dublin: Columba Press).

O'Halloran, J. (2011), *Building Community – Vision and Practice* (Dublin: Currach Press).

O'Hanlon, G. (2011), *A New Vision for the Catholic Church: A View from Ireland* (Dublin: Columba Press).

O'Sullivan, M. (1986), *The Saving Grace Of God's Love As The Basis Of The Option For The Poor In The Theology Of Gustavo Gutiérrez* (Dublin: Milltown Jesuit Library), Unpublished Ph.D. Thesis.

O'Sullivan, M. (2002), *25th Anniversary of the Martyrdom of Rutilio Grande, S. J.* (Dublin: Milltown Jesuit Library).

O'Sullivan, M. (2010), 'Anniversary Tribute to Archbishop Oscar Romero', *Spirituality*, March–April 2010: 103–108.

O'Sullivan, M. (2012), 'Spiritual Capital and the Turn to Spirituality', in O'Sullivan, M. & Flanagan B. (eds.), *Spiritual Capital: Spirituality in Practice in Christian Perspective* (Surrey: Ashgate Publishing Ltd.).

Pearce, J. (1981), *Under the Eagle* (Boston: South End Press).

Petrella, I. (2006) *The Future of Liberation Theology, An Argument and Manifesto* (London: SCM Press).

Pope Francis: Audience with the media representatives, 2013, [online], available: http://www.news.va/en/news/pope-francis-oh-how-i-wish-for-a-church-that-is-poor, [16 May 2013].

Pope Francis (2013), 'A Big Heart Open To God', in Spadaro A. (ed.), *America – The National Catholic Review* [online] (New York: St. John's University), 1–14.

Pope Francis (2013), *Pope Francis – The Authorised Biography*, in Rubin S. & Ambrogetti, F. (eds.), (London: Hodder and Stoughton).

Pope Francis (2013), *Evangelii Gaudium – Apostolic Exhortations on the Proclamation of the Gospel in Today's World* (Dublin: Veritas).

Puebla: Third General Conference of Latin American Bishops (1979), *Puebla, Evangelisation at Present and in the Future of Latin America, Conclusions* (Washington D.C.: Conference of Catholic Bishops).

Rahner, K. (1979), *The Spirit in the Church* (New York: The Seabury Press).

Rahner, K. (1979), 'Towards a Fundamental Theological Interpretation of Vatican II', *Theological Studies*, 40, 716–727.

Rahner, K. (1983), 'Basic Communities', *Theological Investigations*, *XIX* (London: Darton, Longman & Todd), 159–165.

Rahner, K. (1992), 'On the Holy Spirit', in Kelly, B. (ed.), *Karl Rahner: Theologian of the Graced Search for Meaning*, (Minneapolis: Fortress Press), 218–254.

Rahner, K. (1992), 'On Christian Faith, Praxis, and Martyrdom', in Kelly, B. (ed.), *Karl Rahner: Theologian of the Graced Search for Meaning* (Minneapolis: Fortress Press), 298–333.

Redmond, M. (2011), 'Omega: the People's Voice – reflection on Parish Consultation', *The Furrow*, 62 (2), 73–78.

Romero, O. (1978), 'Monseñor Oscar A. Romero: Supensamiento', *Publicaciones Pastorales Arzobispado*, 5, 327.

Romero, O. (1985), *Archbishop Oscar Romero, Voice of the Voiceless: The Four Pastoral Letters and Other Statements* (New York: Orbis Books).

Russell, L. (1974), *Human Liberation in a Feminist Perspective – A Theology* (Philadelphia: Westminster Press).

Schillebeeckx, E. (1990), *Church: The Human Face of God* (New York: Crossroad Publishing Company).

Segundo, J. L. (1973), *The Community Called Church* trans. Drury, J. (New York: Orbis Publications).

Segundo, J. L. (1973), *Grace and The Human Condition – a theology for a new humanity* (New York: Orbis Publications).

Simson, P. (2000), *The Buttonhole Gospels* (Dublin, Partners in Faith).

Sobrino, J. (1979), 'The Significance Of Puebla For The Catholic Church In Latin America', trans. Drury, J. in Eagleson, J. & Scharper. P. (eds.), *Puebla And Beyond* (New York: Orbis Publications).

Sobrino, J. (1984), *The True Church and the Poor* (New York: Orbis Publications).

Sobrino, J. (1985), *Spirituality of Liberation – Towards Political Holiness* (New York: Orbis Publications).

Sobrino, J. (1990), *Archbishop Romero – Memories and Reflections* (New York: Orbis Publications).

Sobrino, J. (1993), 'Central Position of the Reign of God in Liberation Theology', trans. Barr, R. in Ellacuría, I. & Sobrino, J. (eds.), *Systematic Theology: Perspectives from Liberation Theology* (New York: Orbis Publications) 38–74.

Sobrino, J. (1993), 'Spirituality and the Following of Jesus', trans. Barr, R. in Ellacuría, I. & Sobrino, J. (eds.), *Systematic Theology: Perspectives from Liberation Theology*, (New York: Orbis Publications), 233–256.

Sobrino, J. (2008), *No Salvation Outside The Poor. Prophetic-Utopian Essays* (New York: Orbis Publications).

Social Justice Ireland (2012), *Shaping Ireland's Future – Securing Economic Development, Social Equity and Sustainability*, in Healy, S., Mallon, S., Murphy, M. and Reynolds, B. (eds.) (Dublin: Social Justice Ireland).

Tepedino, A. M. and Ribeiro Brandão, M. (1993), 'Women and the Theology of Liberation', *Myseterium Libertionis – Functional concept of liberation theology*, in Ellacuría, I. & Sobrino, J. (eds.) (New York: Orbis Publications).

Vanier, J. (1979), *Community and Growth* (London: Darton, Longman and Todd).

Waller, J. C. (2010), 'The Spirituality of the Saint Vincent de Paul Society', *Spirituality*, 16 (88), 46–49.

Wresinski, J. (2002), *The Poor are the Church: A Conversation with Fr. Joseph Wresinski, Founder of the Fourth World Movement*, in Anouil, G. (ed.), (Mystic CT: Twenty-Third Publications).